Literate

R.I.P.
BILL RUSSELL
1934-2022

Shown here to the right of teammate K.C. Jones (1932-2020), Bill Russell was one of the most dominate basketball players of all time. He followed up consecutive national championships with the San Francisco Dons (1955 and 1956) with a gold medal in the 1956 Olympics. In a 13-year career with the Boston Celtics, Russell almost always came out on top in the end, winning a staggering 11 NBA championships. From 1966 to 1969, he played and coached the Celtics, becoming the first Black head coach in NBA history. Throughout all of it, he championed civil rights.

Foreword

Heat of the Moment
William Meiners

I don't know that these are the worst of times. Though they may be among the most absurd. And for the longest time, I never figured *I* was living through history. At the start of this century I conferred with colleagues who came of age in the 1980s about "fighting for our right to party." The historical stuff happened in our parents' and grandparents' lives.

In July 1995, I lived through a heat catastrophe in Chicago. I remember the elevated temps and news accounts of people dying in it. But I had a window-unit air conditioner and got by just fine. I probably partied pretty hard throughout the week while hardly rising from a barstool at Gunther Murphy's on Belmont. The history, however, which only deemed it a weather disaster in the aftermath, was made over a five-day period with more than 700 heat-related deaths in the city.

I watched a lot of history unfold on television, yet for years the only reality TV I sought was sports. In those same Chicago days of mine, a split screen showcased both the O.J. chase and an NBA finals game. When I landed a job as a writing propagandist for Purdue University, I purchased my first large-screen TV. Mainly for sports, but I watched 9/11 go down live, tuned in for the aftermath of a mass shooting on Virginia Tech's campus, and started watching more of the satirists who lampooned politicians who increasingly made Washington D.C. seem more akin to the *Morton Downey Jr. Show*.

In the dumpster fire of these Trumpian times I'm reminded how much I hated Morton Downey Jr. and the other reality television that rebranded a lecherous businessman who bankrupted a casino, who lifted his profile through racism and attacks on "the other." And the heat is only rising with him out of office, barring any consequence for Agent Orange unleashing his hillbillies "to the Capitol!" in a failed coup d'état.

On highly defined televisions in our modest Michigan home, I seem to be searching for some news from the homeland of sanity, wishful for reruns from a time when I didn't care about politics. So it's more MSNBC and CNN than SportsCenter for me. I listen to NPR in the shower. I read books on the rising tide of fascism (not for fun), and by disillusioned Republicans wondering where it all went wrong, and about an 1898 insurrection in Wilmington, North Carolina, that bears eerie resemblance to January 6.

In a divided nation — with rifts between states red and blue, cable news feuds, and misinformation minefields — it all seems like sport. The high-volume radio rant kind. And a blood sport with all the violent rhetoric you can applaud or abhor from the front-row seat of your Lazy Boy.

Amidst all this angst and unease, I figured *Sport Literate* should get a little louder. It ain't all a game of catch with Dad. We put out a call for a "social justice" contest and I believe you will see how Sydney Lea and Mark Lupinetti answered those calls splendidly. Virginia Ottley Craighill, our guest judge for the essays, has her own insightful take on how Lea stood out among the anonymous finalists.

Frank Van Zant, in choosing his favorite poem, said Lupinetti and a couple of close seconds "are artful in what they do not do," with nothing overstated, nothing over-explained. "In fact, it is an absence of something that catches the breath — an empty bus seat, an obstructed view," Frank said. "The absence fills us with questions and wonder for the full drama and back story. Will there be loss? A tragedy? What is extraordinary in what we take for granted?"

In a couple of historical essays, one *SL* writer examines rugby through years of South African apartheid and two others explore the bygone Eastern Basketball League, which spurred integration into the NBA. There are some tough truths told from two different writers on the subject of sexual assault. And it probably wouldn't be *Sport Literate* without some baseball poetry and prose — enough for a lineup as a reflective nine takes you out to the ballgame.

Even as a small press publisher, I am proud to lift the voices of these poets and writers. And whether you're troubled by the times, or just ducking out of the extreme heat, I hope you'll find someone who speaks to you.

William Meiners is the founding editor of *Sport Literate*. His book, *Though the Odds Be Great or Small*, cowritten with Terry Brennan, was published by Loyola Press in August 2021. He is a reporter, teacher, and family man in the middle of Michigan.

Volume 15, Issue 1

William Meiners
Editor

Frank Van Zant
Poetry Editor

Nicholas Reading
Assistant Editor

Brian McKenna
Assistant Editor

Michael Gawdzik
Assistant Editor

Erin Ingram
Designer

Elizabeth Embrey
Website Editor

Molly Meiners
Social Media Specialist

Glenn Guth
Mouthpiece

KDP
Printer

Sport Literate™ is a literary journal published by Pint-Size Publications, a nonprofit corporation. We feature creative nonfiction, poetry, and interviews. Individual subscription rates are $20 for two issues, domestic; $60 for two issues, foreign; and $30 for two issues, libraries and institutions. We publish two issues per year. If you're already a subscriber but moving, please send us your address change by emailing billsportliterate@gmail.com.

> Please note the address of our Michigan headquarters.
> *Sport Literate*
> William Meiners
> 1422 Meadow Street
> Mount Pleasant, MI 48858

We welcome poetry and all types of creative nonfiction (personal essays, literary journalism, travel pieces, etc.) that fall within our broad definition of sport. You may query with interview or photo essay ideas. **All submissions must come through the Submittable tool on our website**. Check out archived work there, spring for a recent issue, and send your best work our way.

Support

SL YOUR NAME HERE

As we begin Volume XV, we would like to thank all the *Sport Literate* backers who have renewed their support of our publications. Some of you have been with us since 1995! We're also happy to welcome those new names into the fold, which will appear here for two issues. To continue supporting this unique small press offering, please make your tax-deductible donation in one of the categories below.

Franchise Players ($500)
Pinch Hitters ($100)
Bench Warmers ($66)

Franchise Players
Mick and Kris Meiners, Anonymous (for Bob and Eileen Meiners)

Pinch Hitters
Michael Burke, William Daniels, Susan Eleuterio, Patrick and Beth Gavaghan, Benedict Giamo, John Girardi, Glenn and Kathleen Guth, Doug and Courtney Howie, Lance Mason, Meiners-Schmeltz Family, Virginia Mend, Karl and Barb Meyer, David Sisneros Jr., Mark Wukas

Bench Warmers
Marty Allen, Terri Kirby Erickson (in memory of Anders Folke Erickson and Tom Kirby), James Fisher, Chuck Lima

Sport Literate falls under the umbrella of Pint-Size Publications, a nonprofit corporation. Checks, made payable to *Sport Literate*, can be sent to the Michigan home office, care of Mr. Bill. PayPal users can send money to: **billsportliterate@gmail.com.**

Sport Literate
William Meiners
1422 Meadow Street
Mount Pleasant, MI 48858

Subscribe, donate, or peruse online at www.sportliterate.org.

TABLE OF CONTENTS

Hot Summer 2022   Volume 15, Issue 1

Who's on First
8 **John S. O'Connor:** Defining Moments

Poetry
20 **Kathleen Williamson:** When We Were the Visiting Team
22 **Ben Giamo:** Municipal Stadium

Essays
24 **Richard Holinger:** Coach
30 **Carol W. Runyan:** Anything Unusual?

Rugby History
36 **Lance Mason:** A Long Road Home: Getting There from Here

SL Social Justice Contest
42 **Sydney Lea:** The Cardinal, the Cops, and the Say-Hey Kid
48 **Virginia Ottley Craighill:** On the Winning Essay
50 **Flavian Mark Lupinetti:** Wrestling Lake Burn

SL Football
52 **Michael Graham:** NFL Road Trip
56 **John Monagle:** After the Catch
58 **Remi Recchia:** Football Tailgate as Anthropology: Field Notes

Pint-Size Publications
EST 1995

Our fathers, mostly professionals — doctors, lawyers, presidents of companies — surely welcomed anyone with a heartbeat to lead their sons in the Scout pledge and to take them on overnight hikes.
    Richard Holinger

The second great war had ended a mere six years before, and while this was an eternity to a small child, it was an eyeblink to my father, who had commanded a company of so-called Colored Troops during that epical conflict.
    Sydney Lea

SL **Basketball**
60 Syl Sobel & Jay Rosenstein: Blackballed: Race, the NBA, and the Eastern Professional Basketball League
68 Flavian Mark Lupinetti: Three at Home, Four on the Road, Five When You're Behind

SL **Tennis**
70 Pam Sinicrope: We Know the Truth About Bones; That's When You Know

SL **Baseball**
72 Kate Wylie: 1932
74 Todd Morgan: The List
78 Kent Jacobson: Mrs. Talbot and a Field
82 Leland Seese: Referred Pain
84 Jason Koo: Swearing in the Suburbs
98 Bill Gruber: Pitching Lessons
106 Alinda Wasner: Obstructed View: Love and Baseball
107 Matthew Sisson: An Appearance of Brightness
108 Jeffrey Alfier: Autumn Field in a Pascagoula Sundown

Our little town's neighborhoods were segregated. Our elementary schools too. Our only public swimming pool never dampened a black body.
— Flavian Mark Lupinetti

The day the elephants marched through Corktown and down Michigan Avenue, the crowds going wild inside Tiger Stadium with Gibby at bat and us in our obstructed view seats where we couldn't see diddly but what did that matter because we were crazy in love...
— Alinda Wasner

Who's on First

Defining Moments
John S. O'Connor

As Howard Cosell often said, "Let me take you back." The Houston Astrodome. September 20, 1973: The Battle of the Sexes tennis match between Billie Jean King and Bobby Riggs. I watched with my whole family, a rare event in our household. Dad and Mom in their mismatched easy chairs, and my two sisters and brother on the sagging sofa, while I lay on the floor, propping my head up with my hand, as I spent much of my childhood: watching TV.

Cosell was perhaps best known for his coverage of Muhammad Ali, and his presence was meant to lend a certain pugilistic gravitas to this "slug fest," a match he called with Billie Jean's doubles partner, Rosie Casals. Cosell opened the coverage by saying, "The moment the country has been waiting for has finally arrived." This hype was largely borne out by the ratings afterward: over 90 million people watched the match world-wide, over 60 million Americans. King's victory was a huge triumph for women and seemed to fulfill the promise of Title IX legislation passed the year before. But only now, in retrospect, can I see how much that event, and the sports heroes of my youth, came to shape the rest of my life as well.

Though Houston was only about 1,000 miles away from Chicago, the match might as well have been played on the moon considering how impossibly far away the match was from my experience. Yet, somehow, special athletes can make such defining moments immediate and personally affecting.

I had just turned nine in 1973, and fourth grade had just started, when that match was played. We had recently moved to what we called a "white neighborhood" on the Northwest side of Chicago where my parents had bought their first and only house. Dad always said we were the last white family to leave the West side, at the tail end of the "white flight," and at the time I took it literally. I pictured my parents and my older siblings carrying what they could — suitcases and stuffed animals in their arms, dented saucepans and a charred tea kettle balanced on their heads — as they climbed aboard the last rickety truck ambling north on Austin Blvd., an image I must have summoned from re-runs of *The Beverly Hillbillies*.

Actually what Dad said was that we had left "the jungle," which stung even then since my best friend until the move was a Black boy named Skookie. I guess Dad didn't mind my playing with an African-American boy while I was still very young. My older siblings had already internalized the invisible boundaries of race, which were perhaps not so invisible in what has consistently been one of the most segregated cities in the U.S. I later found out that Skookie's real name was Benjamin Moore, but in the late 1960s I guess not even Benjamin Moore provided a broad enough color palette to allow for thinking beyond black and white.

To shut me up, I'm sure, and to give themselves some time and space to settle us in to the new house, my parents bought me a used tennis racquet from a second-hand sporting goods store about a mile from our new house. The racquet was a genuine Rawlings Brian Fairlie autographed model (What? You haven't heard of him? He was the New Zealander who partnered with Frew McMillan to make it all the way to the doubles semi-finals at the 1967 French Open. Seriously? That's all it took for a pro to get their own "autograph" tennis racquet in the days before the tennis explosion?).

I spent most of my childhood hitting a tennis ball against a giant brick wall: the parking lot of The Ice House, a carpeting warehouse at the end of my block that was once the home of The Jefferson Ice Company. The stenciled name of the former tenant sat right next to the loading dock. Even though the company had been gone for years, everyone in the neighborhood still called that building The Ice House, grateful for a recognizable place marker in the bland brick breadth of "the bungalow belt."

Nearly every afternoon of my boyhood was spent hitting tennis balls against the wall. I played in the rain, and, in the winter months, I even brought a shovel with me to clear away a clean rectangle of "court space." As a mediocre tournament player, and a guy who eventually peaked as a bottom-rung player on a University of Chicago D-III team, it was clear to me early on (though probably not as early as it should have been), that the Ice House wall was the closest I'd ever get to playing in a Grand Slam tennis tournament. For me, you see, The Ice House was Forest Hills and Flushing Meadows of the U.S. Open; Kooyong Stadium down under; the slow red clay of Roland Garros. Christ, to me, The Ice House was the All-England Lawn Tennis Club at Wimbledon.

At first I mostly tried to break "world records" of consecutive volleys off the wall, and later I imitated the Battle of the Sexes match and the WCT finals, just about the only tennis then shown on TV. But the following year, when Chrissy Evert and Jimmy Connors won Wimbledon, I went crazy for the sport altogether, playing not just matches against that wall but entire draws of Grand Slam championships.

Just how tennis-crazy was I? Well, when Sister Benigna asked us to write "friendly letters," every other kid in class chose to write to a relative. I chose Rosie Casals. At first Sister said no, but I won her over when I told her how I much I admired the fact that Rosie could win despite being so short — like I was.

Sister said I could write to Ms. Casals (actually she said "Miss Casals"; even then I knew the difference) if I could find her address. From a copy of *World Tennis* magazine, I found out Rosie's home town but not her street address, so I wrote to her, care of the magazine. Sister said she sent all the letters on the same day, and about a month later, when everyone shared the letters they got back, I had nothing to share. Rosie never wrote me back.

Sister gave it an A- since I misspelled Casals' hometown as "San Maeto."

"It's actually San Mateo," she said.

"I don't think so," I remember saying, furious that a nun would challenge my tennis knowledge. This was my area of expertise.

But she quickly played her trump card. "No, it's San Mateo, as in Saint Matthew," she said. "The town was named for a gospel writer just like you were."

I was lucky to choose tennis — or perhaps it chose me. I mean, think of the historical dominos falling here: 1972, the year Title IX became law; 1973, the year of the Battle of the Sexes match, the year of Arthur Ashe's historic visit to Apartheid-ruled South Africa, and the year I got my first tennis racquet; 1974, the year tennis exploded in popularity due in large part to the marketing dream couple of Chrissy Evert and Jimmy Connors; and the spring of 1975 when the U.S. finally left Vietnam and McFetridge, the first ever indoor Chicago Park District tennis facility, opened — predictably, in retrospect, on the North side. Two months later King and Ashe won Wimbledon. You may think I am trivializing historical events here by intertwining them with my own paltry sports exploits, but looking back they all now seem connected. Like most people I'd guess, I once thought of history as a past tense enterprise, but, as James Baldwin said, "History is not the past. It is the present. We carry our history with us. We are our history" — we as a nation and each of us individually.

I used to think of those practice wall sessions — thousands of hours in my childhood — as sort of pathetic, solipsistic "alone time." Staring at a wall even as I walled-off the world around me. But now in my mind's eye, I see myself a little like Roddy Doyle's Paddy Clarke who, as a Dublin boy at about the same age says, "Sometimes, when you were thinking about something, trying to understand it, it opened up in your head without you expecting it to, like it was a soft spongy light unfolding and you understood, it made sense forever."

When I was in fourth grade, Dad drank more than ever and beat my older brother Mike almost every week. Since Mike and I shared a room, I had a front row seat, often hiding under the sheets or crouching behind the radiator to shield myself from the violent spectacle of my dad, a construction worker who was nicknamed Big Mike by his fellow laborers, beating my skinny and shaking brother with his work pants' belt.

We were sensitive as seismologists to my father's approach, anticipating his presence long before we saw his face. We'd listen for the breaking and jerking of his Impala outside, and the heavy thud of his construction boots on the front steps — powerful signs of what would come next, the way horror movie directors show roadside puddles shivering with every footfall long before the monster actually appears.

My father always entered our house the same way: swinging the front door open to crash against the little writing desk on which no one ever wrote. Then he'd slam the door shut behind him so hard that the portrait of St. Theresa, the Little Flower, swung back and forth on the penny nail peg, as if she were shaking her head in disapproval. The fights always ended in one of two ways: Dad would pass out or he'd drive off for the Six Penny Bit and, when he left, our house once again grew cold and quiet as ice.

My own schoolwork suffered mightily that year. In the late fall, I hadn't turned in any assignments for about a month, and I started to smell at school. I slept in my Catholic school uniform, and I didn't change my clothes for a week. We didn't have a washing machine, and we only did laundry on the weekends when my mom and sisters took piles of laundry in shopping carts down to The Washing Well, the local laundromat.

With Dad's drinking and Mom working two or three part-time jobs as a "private nurse" to elderly patients, many suffering from dementia, some of my basic needs went unsupervised. One day Mrs. Regal, my teacher, broached these subjects with me. She told me I could move down a level if I found the material too difficult. I was hurt. Reading "with fluency" was always my favorite part of school. I spent large parts of every day in the classroom daydreaming until it was my turn again to read a paragraph. How could she possibly think it was too hard all of a sudden?

I didn't respond at all. I stared at my sneakers. Then she told me I had begun to carry an odor. I was shocked, mortified. She tried to be comforting, and told me that her husband, Mr. Regal, sometimes smelled bad, especially if he wore the same underwear on consecutive days.

Luckily that classroom was held in a mobile home trailer next to the school because I have never in my life wanted to jump out a window more. I couldn't believe my ears. Why was she telling me about the pee stains in her husband's boxers?

If there was no clean laundry around, I'd rinse my underwear with bar soap under the bathroom faucet before heading off to school. To make up ground in my reading work, I took advantage of the SRA reading program, a self-directed program color-coded by levels of achievement. Rather than ever talk about Mr. Regal's foul-smelling drawers again, I became feverishly self-directed and finished the entire fourth-grade curriculum in a few weeks. While I can offer no data to support the idea, I am convinced that we would be a nation of readers if all children were pulled aside during their formative years and given an explicit talk about the nethergarments of their teacher's spouse.

Sports once again saved me. For independent bonus reading, I chose a new series of short American sports bios and devoured them all. I read the tennis players first (Billie Jean King and Maureen Connolly; Arthur Ashe and Pancho Gonzalez), but I read the entire series soon enough: Muhammad Ali, Lee Trevino, Jim Plunkett, Sandy Koufax, Jim Thorpe, and Mickey Mantle. Even the boring sports like golf. I couldn't get enough of the sports books. My mom and sisters used to go to the Mayfair Public Library every couple of weeks and bring back shopping carts full of books, but before those sports books I was sure the library had nothing of interest for me.

So, when Mrs. Regal suggested I could use extra reading practice, I waited for the right moment — after dad had gone on yet another rant — and, finding Mom crying in the kitchen, I talked her into subscribing to *Tennis* and *World Tennis* magazines, which we got at a student rate. And every day when school let out, I'd grab my racquet and "re-play" the matches I'd read about against The Ice House wall or use the world rankings at the back to create full Grand Slam draws.

I even read the tennis rulebook over and over again. The rules settled all ambiguity as clearly as the white lines on a tennis court demarcated the service boxes, baselines, and alleys. Tennis provided an abundance of order and stability, the very commodities that were most missing in my home life.

You can tell a lot about a person from the sports figures they choose to admire. King and Ashe and Ali were at the top of my list. Okay, in fairness I also loved Pete Rose and Jimmy Connors, "brash" athletes (read: assholes) who loved crashing into things and others in order to get noticed, who bragged about outworking everyone around them, who pursued their goals relentlessly. But in tennis particularly, Ashe and King offered a different kind of sports model than you could find anywhere else in sport. They were bespectacled, pensive, cogent. They cared about ideas and causes that were bigger than themselves.

As my tennis skills plateaued, I threw myself more fully into academic pursuits, eventually becoming a high school English teacher. Unable to match their athleticism, I attempted to follow their moral example. Like Mrs. Regal did in her own way, I have tried to expand the narrow confines of the literary canon and even the definition of "literary study" to represent all of humanity: books by women, writers of color, LGBTQ authors, neuro-diverse authors, films, podcasts, graphic novels — any text that might personally engage students and introduce them to the ongoing spectacle of human history to which everyone must be invited.

My father never got to play sports of any kind, having left school in Ireland in the second grade to work full time for his family. But he watched sports on TV when he was home. He liked boxing most of all — Muhammad Ali was the only black man I ever heard him praise — but I don't think he understood any of the American sports he watched. He rooted mostly for the Irish players, the Fighting Irish, of course, but also, smitten by the shamrock logo on their warmup suits, he cheered on the Boston Celtics (which he pronounced KELL-tics) as if they were his home team, later insisting, for example, that Cedric "Cornbread" Maxwell was from "the old country." (I knew a Maxwell back in Connemara). When watching tennis with my father, on those rare occasions when I'd watch with him, I only recall him shouting, "Who won that one?" While smashing a fist into an open palm after — and sometimes during — each point. My father never in his life set foot on a tennis court. He never saw me play.

 The one sport Dad knew better than me was boxing. It was nice for once to cheer for the same guy, Muhammad Ali. I'm not sure why he loved Ali so much when he seemed to hate or fear black people in general. Maybe it was Ali's braggadocio, maybe his disregard for authority (the reason he liked Johnny Cash). But he let me buy a 45 of "Muhammad, the Black Superman," which I played constantly and sang non-stop.

 The other song I played out that year was "Philadelphia Freedom," the Elton John song written for Billie Jean's World Team Tennis project. All summer I rode my bike no-handed around the block about 50 times a day, singing that song — until the neighborhood rebelled. On one of my many circuits, kids from down the block who were sick of hearing that song jumped off their porches and blocked my path. "Shut up," they said. "Quit singing that stupid Elton John song."

 "Why should I? He's great, he even wrote that song for Billie Jean King."

"He's a faggot. The guy's even admitted he's a bisexual. It was in the paper."

I don't think any of us knew what those terms even meant. It was the filthiest thing I had ever heard. "He is not," I protested before starting to cry.

And then, seeing me upset, a bunch of kids started up a mocking sing-song chant: "EL-ton JOHN is bi-SEX-u-al. BILL-ie Jean KING is bi-SEX-u-al." It probably only lasted a couple of minutes, but it seemed interminable. Picture the prom scene from Carrie minus the pigs' blood. I rode my bike back home, humiliated and confused. "What's wrong?" Mom asked but I couldn't tell her. That language was too disgusting. Instead, I did what I always did. I went down to The Ice House for a few hours and played an entire season of World Team Tennis. The Philadelphia Freedoms, who actually lost in the first ever WTT title, won my re-creation, behind the solid play of team captain Billie Jean King, the Australian legend Fred Stolle, and the surprisingly strong play of New Zealander, Brian Fairlie.

I think about that "mocking chant" incident every time one of my students (five this year alone) is hospitalized for self-harm or attempted suicide, especially when they never quite fit into the "traditional" gender binary. And, of course, I think so often of those students over the years who killed themselves when the world could not, or would not, accommodate their differences: their sexual orientation or their neurodiversity or their mental illness.

A few years ago, in the middle of a class in which we were studying Ta-Nehisi Coates' *Between the World and Me*, a student asked me a question which stunned me: "What has been the biggest change in your lifetime?" I'm usually hesitant to make such pronouncements, and I explained that differences I've noted may not be the same for everyone, but something about that question prompted a moment of clarity for me. "Changing definitions," I said. Maybe that's always the case in every succeeding generation, but it feels more profound now. Together we made a list on the board: changing definitions of gender, of marriage, of love, of race, of religion, of mental illness, of equity, of family, of alcoholism. ("It's not him," Mom always said. "It's his disease.")

The word "definition" comes to us from Latin: to set boundaries to. The limit, the *fin*, the end point, the edge, the demarcation line, the wall. Boundaries that were once thought to be as solid as a brick wall, have become a little looser. To some, I think, it can feel like the very architecture of the world is crumbling, but the structures are not merely collapsing, they are being reconstructed, our lives re-imagined. And without those rigid walls there may be more points of access for everyone, more avenues of opportunity for freedom, self-definition, and self-determination.

I ended up meeting Ali and King, but not Arthur Ashe. I met Billie Jean King at the Virginia Slims tennis tournament held in Chicago when I was about 12. The tournament was held at the Chicago Amphitheater in the old stockyards district, perhaps my first foray to the South Side. I went several nights that week. The first night my mother took me and, since she did not drive for another 25 years until my after Dad had died, we took a long 'L' ride and a CTA bus to get down there. The other nights I mooched a ride off my friend and doubles partner Kevin, whose family frequently drove me to matches.

While Kevin and I were running around the tournament grounds, we passed the broadcasting booth where Billie Jean King was calling the action while she recuperated from yet another knee injury. Billie Jean actually let us fetch her cups of water during the evening matches. The 1975 Wimbledon singles champion actually let Kevin, his brother, and me supply her with tiny paper cups of water for hours until she finally put an end to the madness and the comical array of half-full Dixie cups spread out before her.

At that tournament a few of us also got to serve as unrequested ball boys at practice matches, scrambling and bowing in deference to players when they were ready to serve. That way I got to see many pro players up close — including Sue Barker, the young star from Devonshire, England, whom I had just read about in *World Tennis* magazine ("The Cream Rises to the Top") and on whom I had a bit of a crush; and Rosie Casals, though I chickened out of asking her why she had never responded to my letter.

The most memorable encounter by far — and a story I milked to fellow tennis players for years afterward — was ball-boying a doubles practice set that included Renee Richards, the first trans-player to ever play on the tour. Richards towered over everyone, even the flying Dutchwoman, Bette Stove, who was probably 6 feet herself. Richards was 6'3", wore glasses and had effective if awkward looking shots. Born Richard Raskin, a minor pro on the men's tour in the 1960s, Renee Richards accepted her identity as a woman, and played on the pro women's tour 20 years later.

Everyone wanted to hear my story of ball-boying for Renee Richards. What they really wanted was a monster story. I admit I played to the crowd at times, making my (as-yet-unchanged) voice huskier and exaggerating her height by slowly craning my head north as if I were looking up at a skyscraper that just kept on going. But in fact she was kind and patient. She just wanted to play.

Years later I also got to meet Muhammad Ali. In college, my work-study jobs all involved tutoring and after school help at under-resourced public schools on the South Side of Chicago. While working at one of them, I received a message that, at the time, seemed surreal: would I be interested in tutoring kids at the champ's Kenwood mansion? I had to think about this job offer for about two seconds before running to a phone to accept! My best friend — and now wife — Eleni and I had sort of met the champ many times at the University Gardens, a Middle Eastern restaurant on 53rd St., but those encounters were more like brief encounters with royalty. We kept our distance, mouthed hellos, resisted the urge to genuflect, and he smiled, waved generously, and said hello back.

At the time I thought he was ancient, his career long over, but I was later stunned to learn that the champ would have been about 42 at that time. Age is another barrier that seems impossible to bridge when you are very young, but these days 42 seems downright puppyish.

Ali's mansion is still the only house I've ever visited with an elevator. I took it up to the top floor and met two kids in the library. I would have happily tutored them for free (I mean I think I would have, but I certainly didn't!). Visiting my parents on a weekend trip home to the northside — an entire world away — I couldn't wait to tell my parents. I believe it was the proudest my father ever was of me. He didn't say he was proud, but I could tell he thought I might have "actually learned something at those schools of mine." Although I felt bad telling him about the early reading support I was giving to those kids, helping them to read better and more confidently even as I knew my own dad never learned to read.

I never met Ashe, but his example still influenced me deeply. In grade school, when the nuns would ask who we should offer up our daily work for, I was always ready with a cause. Having read of Ashe's historic trip to South Africa, I regularly suggested, "For the people of South Africa struggling under the racist system of Apartheid."

Ashe also offered me the first example of a nerd jock who deeply believed in the power of education. Ashe knew, as chronicled in John McPhee's *Levels of the Game*, that "education reflects a culture's values. If the culture is warped you get a warped education." He was a four-year student-athlete at UCLA, unlike the one-and-doners like Connors and McEnroe, who counted among his personal heroes — alongside Jackie Robinson and Pancho Gonzalez — two Irish-Americans, John and Bobby Kennedy.

Beyond those morning prayers at St. Ed's, I felt Ashe's influence as I worked on the divestiture campaign at the University of Chicago since the school had invested heavily in South Africa's racist government. I wasn't a lead organizer by any stretch, but I showed up for all the meetings, made signs, marched, and protested with thousands of others, and eventually, when the university finally divested, I thought about Arthur Ashe.

As a tennis player I probably peaked in an endless moonball match against DePaul, a meaningless match since the team contest had already been decided. Kevin's brother Mike was on that DePaul team, and their coach, George Lott, was a Grand Slam doubles champ himself. And as my tennis skills levelled off, I concentrated more on academic work.

I went back to work on my undergraduate exams, specializing in Hegel's lectures on the *Philosophy of History*. Why Hegel? Well, the department rule had been that candidates had to read philosophy in the original language. My language had been Spanish, but the department chair explained to me that wouldn't work since "no 'first-rate' philosopher had ever written in Spanish"! I pleaded my case, but my suggestions were shot down as he told me, "Miguel de Unamuno was a third-rate thinker and *Don Quixote* was, in no way, a work of philosophy."

So I pathetically plodded through Hegel in translation (I know no German. Tell no one!). I was especially interested in the idea of historical striving on a national and an individual level, and what Hegel saw as the inevitable unfolding of history. In charting this progress, Hegel referred to world historical figures, like Socrates and Napoleon, who broke from existing systems and structures to promote the consciousness of freedom. In a way, King and Ali and Ashe were like such figures, refusing to be limited by unfair constraints. I, along with many millions of others, was the lucky beneficiary of their example.

My dad stopped speaking to me for five years when I married a "black woman." He did not attend our wedding. Actually, my wife is not black. She is a light-skinned, blonde woman from suburban Philadelphia, who had been adopted into a Greek family. But for my dad the math was damningly clear. She was Greek, and Greeks are Blacks. My dad chose to forget that the Irish were once black, that they, as Ta-Nehisi Coates puts it, were once "drawn in the same ravenous, lustful and simian way." Or maybe he just never knew Coates' truth that "being named 'black' was just someone's name for being at the bottom, a human turned to object, object turned to pariah." Definitions: they'll fuck you every time.

These days, I'm coming to the end of my career teaching English — 35 years and counting (hopefully many more, but you never know). As Ali said, "Don't count the days, make the days count." I'm looking back at the forces that led me to choose this profession. My father and I did end up speaking again for the few years before he died — when he who had always had to be so strong was suddenly frail and vulnerable.

For a while I was content to imagine that I had defined myself as my father's opposite: he worked construction; I majored in philosophy. He was unable to read or write; I got a PhD in English and became a high school English teacher. He faced grim realities head on at an early age, while I happily retreated into the fortress of my imagination — reading books and playing in tennis tournaments, some real, and some the products of my own self-invention.

My dad's inaccessibility led me to fins role models in other arenas — in teachers, coaches, athletes, and authors, people who lived for something bigger than themselves, whose conception of the world was capacious enough to allow for others to follow their example and seek out new paths all their own.

Editorial note: Portions of this essay originally appeared in "The Ice House," published in *Under the Sun* (online).

John S. O'Connor is a public school teacher and an adjunct professor at Northwestern University. He has written two books on the teaching of writing, two books of haiku, and a chapbook of poems. Two previous essays were named Notable in *Best American Essays,* and one also in *Best American Sports Writing.*

Our "Best Americans"

Since our founding in 1995, we've been lucky enough to field more than 30 writers whose *Sport Literate* essays earned notable nods in two "Best American" anthologies. Three republished in *Best American Sports Writing*.

NOTABLE ESSAYS IN *BEST AMERICAN SPORTS WRITING*:
Frank Soos, (three times): "Obituary with Bamboo Fly Rod," 1997, "On His Slowness," 1999, and "Another Kind of Loneliness," 2013; **Mark Wukas**, "Running with Ghosts," 1998; **Molly Moynahan**, "Don't Walk," 2000; **Jay Lesandrini**, "Waiting on Deck," 2010; **Dave Essinger**, "Hallucinating in Suburbia: John Cheever, Buddha, and the Unabomber on the Urban Ultramarathon," 2014; **Alessandra Nolan**, "Channeling Mr. Jordan," 2016; **Laura Legge**, "The Responsible Player," 2017; **Liz Prato**, "Flights of Two," and **Eric Van Meter**, "St. Anthony and Buddha Bike Through the Desert," 2018; **Justina Elias**, "Hard Cut," **Mark Anthony Jarman**, "A Nation Plays Chopsticks," **Michael Kula**, "How to Repair a Bicycle," **John Julius Reel**, "Touched by the Greatest," & **Cinthia Ritchie**, "Random Numbers from a Summer of Alaska Trail Running," 2020.

NOTABLE ESSAYS IN *BEST AMERICAN ESSAYS*:
Michael Steinberg, "Elegy for Ebbets," 2002; **William Huhn**, "The Triple Crown," 2004; **Robert Parker**, "The Running of the Bull," 2006; **Benedict Giamo**, "Played Out," 2009; **Peter Stine**, "Detroit Marathon," 2010; **Cinthia Ritchie**, "Running," 2012; **Katie Cortese**, "Winning Like a Girl," 2014; **Gayle Brandeis**, "IceTown," **Rachel Luria**, "The Rush Gives Warmth Enough," & **Phillip A. Snyder**, "Rental Horses," 2016; **Michael J. Hess**, "On the Morning After the Crash," 2017; **Liz Prato**, "Flights of Two," 2018; **Virginia Ottley Craighhill**, "The Lost Cause," 2019; **Justina Elias**, "Hard Cut," & **William Loizeaux**, "Sin and Baseball," 2020; **Anthony D'Aries**, "No Man's Land," 2021.

REPUBLISHED: *BEST AMERICAN SPORTS WRITING*:
Mark Pearson, "The Short History of an Ear," 2010; **Cinthia Ritchie**, "Running," 2012; **Virginia Ottley Craighhill**, "The Lost Cause," 2019.

Poetry

When We Were the Visiting Team
Kathleen Williamson

When we said their high school sucked
we meant that it looked like a prison —
windows so dirty we wrestled in shadow,
and so skinny even our 96-pounder
couldn't have squeezed through.

It was cold and dank and socks floated
in puddles in the locker room
where half the toilets didn't flush,
and the stench made us breathe
through our mouths.

Splintered bleachers tore at the back
of our thighs and yanked our singlets.
The home team's uniforms had lost
their elasticity and hung loose
where they should have hugged.

The worst of us laughed —
others, so fogged by cravings
for calories and carbs and sex,
couldn't think at all, but a few of us
thought of our school, high on a hill, sun
pouring in windows like a cathedral.

And this memory of us,
basking in the light, anointed,
glistened poison into our empty stomachs.
Here in this murky gym, we felt,
somehow, implicated.

Kathleen Williamson's chapbook *Feather & Bone* will be published by Finishing Line Press this November. She won runner-up prize in the SLAB poetry contest and was a winner in the Poetry in the Pavement project in Sleepy Hollow, New York. Her work has been published in *Ponder Review, Newtown Literary*, and *Lunate* as well other literary journals. After spending countless hours watching her son wrestle, she wrote a young adult novel about high school wrestling and published a short story about that subject in *Inkwell Journal*.

Poetry

Municipal Stadium
Ben Giamo

Hephaestus, a smithing god and celestial artificer, must have hammered it out on the anvil of his Olympus workshop, circa 1930. In the shape of a horseshoe like the ancient Greek *stadion*, though this one — Municipal Stadium — intended for modern times, so the design not as narrow. A period piece fashioned with a covered double-decked grandstand and lower level in the familiar U formation, for the metropolitan populace had grown over the millennia, especially in the Rust Belt of the New World. Seating capacity 81,000, swelling at times to 86,000 with standing room, as witnessed in the fifth game of the 1948 World Series.

With the Herculean help of the gods, and their gigantic ropes and pulleys, Heph lowered the stadium gradually through layers of heavenly and earthly atmospheres, setting down the stone, steel, and cement structure gently on the grounds of a lakefront landfill. Used cars and tires — the detritus of an industrial age. Coordinates as follows: 41.5061 degrees N., 81.6995 degrees W. It was a promising site despite the Erie location. All Heph asked in exchange for his divine labor were season tickets in perpetuity for home baseball and football games. Agreed upon with a sacrifice: forty-two steel columns holding up the whole weight of the sports world, and blocking the view of many unsuspecting ticketholders seated behind the majestic rivets.

The bewilderment of the eyes awaits as you stroll by the stone façade and enter the stadium gate, making your way up the broad ramp to the cavernous concourse of concession stands. You look up for the section that matches the numbers on your ticket stub. There. You turn and begin walking through the opening, up or down the aisle to find your seat. Here you cross a blessed threshold — sunlight pouring onto the geometry of the contest; a square tipped into a diamond for one game, and a gridiron laid down along the emerald garden from center field fence to home plate for the other. Impossible to play both games at once. That is why we have seasons.

The playing fields authored by the god of leisure and order. No shadows, reflections, and illusions as in the cave. No, here everything is out in the open — the buoyant light of the visible world, all objects perceived by the senses and a mind bent on resolving the *agon* on favorable terms. The crowd's face might look like silly putty, but ever so serious is its relentless roar: Go Tribe! Go Browns! Bring home the justice — beauty — truth — and goodness. Always. The ascent beckons.

Until time's up, circa 1995, and the downward pull into ignorance intrudes again. Now the demolition, extinguishing the light, exchanging mercy for greed. Sorry Heph, nothing lasts forever in these mere mortal parts. After Bob Hope sings a homemade version of "Thanks for the Memory," the stadium crumbles by vice of the wrecking ball. Goodnight, four NFL Championships. Safe passage, World Series victory. Farewell, ten-cent beer night. So long, rock concerts. Adieu, athletes who brought so much happiness and grief to a city, a people, a mass transit of human forms transported by foot, by car, by train, by bus, by radio and television, spilling the beads of their collective necklace along the pathways to Mecca.

Much of the demolition debris — 15,000 short tons — was dumped into the lake, where they took root in several artificial reefs just offshore. Beneath the waves, ragged claws and mermaids mingle. The traces of so many heroes wreathed with green seaweed. Their feats remain underwater — bubbling up into the cry of gulls.

Ben Giamo is an emeritus professor of American Studies at Notre Dame University. He is the author of several books: *On the Bowery: Confronting Homelessness in American Society; Beyond Homelessness: Frames of Reference; The Homeless of Ironweed; Kerouac, the Word and the Way: Prose Artist as Spiritual Quester; Notes from the Bowery;* and *Homeless Come Home: An Advocate, the Riverbank, and Murder in Topeka, Kansas.*

Essay

Coach

Richard Holinger

We called him Coach. "Mister Michaelson" (not his real name) preferred the informal moniker. Made him more lovable, I guess. A former U.S. Marine, at six-two or three, about 300 to 350 pounds, squinty eyes peering out from a face bulbous as a bulldog's, he may have counted on such intimacy so that we might warm to him.

Because he looked mean, we feared him. Because we feared him, we wanted his attention. Because we wanted his attention, if he befriended a friend of ours, we got jealous.

He coached our school's seventh grade football team. Being one of the tallest and heaviest (not to mention severely myopic, with thick, heavy glasses) boys, I played guard, expected to destroy my mirror image and tackle the opposing team's quarterback. However, because I hated football, I was no good at it; I only wanted to impress the girls in our class I fell in love with.

One afternoon, Coach addressed my lethargic, disinterested play. "Holinger, you hit like a baby. Next play, knock Sanders on his ass."

Everybody loved that. He had said "ass," in our privileged, white, upper-class world, an off-limits swear word adults must not know we knew. To hear it spoken, well, that kicked ass.

No way in hell I could move "Sanders" or anyone else more than a few inches. Maybe, I thought, the kid would fake a pratfall, even swear at me for hitting him so vehemently.

"Hut!" yelled the quarterback. I charged, backing up Sanders as far as I could the Statue of Liberty.

"Again!" Coach barked.

"Hut!" I rammed a shoulder pad into my doppelganger, but Sanders merely looking bored, even embarrassed.

Coach roared, "You don't knock him down, I'm gonna show you how it's done."

"Hut!" I lunged forward with all the force of a foxtrot lead.

Coach took Sanders' place. Beady eyes bore into mine. I read the disgust of my timidity, of my refusal to annihilate. Coach didn't need helmet, shoulder pads, padded pants, or cleats to educate a rich, fat slob who didn't do shit in practice. He wanted to hurt me so badly that I could not pretend to be hurt. He wanted to loosen something in me that would never adhere again.

"Hike the ball," Coach said.

"Hut!"

Something like a barrel punched me upward and backward. After what seemed like a few minutes in flight, I landed hard.

"Get up," Coach ordered. "You're not hurt. Now do that to Sanders."

Standing up took all my strength. My eyes welled with tears. I got down in my stance, but after the play, Sanders stood tall. I expected another lesson, but Coach had moved on. He'd had his revenge on the big-ass boy whose family could afford an elite independent school that paid him only enough to afford a one-room apartment.

I know that, because one day I saw where he lived.

Why he took us is lost now. We climbed the stairs in a square brick apartment building, where he led us down a dark, bare hall, unlocked a door, and showed us into a room that fit little more than a single unmade bed. If I had known the word, "squalid" would have come to mind. The room's loneliness, its disarray, its odor, repulsed and frightened me. It was my first encounter with poverty. Three of his rooms would fit into the bedroom my brother and I shared. His "apartment" was more den, lair, a place an animal goes for shelter, not for comfort or love.

Once inside, I couldn't keep the room from working me over, its unimaginable performances inside bombarding me with hazy, confusing possibilities. My naïve, pre-adolescent mind tried to fend off the sordid shadow world, but its darkness holds me still.

It shouldn't have; after all, Coach Michaelson was our Boy Scout leader.

He replaced "Pop," an archetypal father figure: bald head, kind face, diminutive build. While delivering wisdom and stories around a campfire, he would occasionally draw on a pipe. He did everything rhythmically, gracefully.

When Pop retired, Coach was hired. The 1950s did not offer the vetting of today's more cautious world. Our fathers, mostly professionals — doctors, lawyers, presidents of companies — surely welcomed anyone with a heartbeat to lead their sons in the Scout pledge and to take them on overnight hikes. As an ex-Marine, who better to survive and corral a pack of blossoming pubescent boys?

There was no assistant scoutmaster for overnights and week-long journeys. Occasionally a father (never a mother) tagged along on a camping trip if the weather predicted sun and the scenery promised woods and a lake, but surely our dads were overjoyed to be rid of us, their weekend blessed with one fewer child.

After encountering Coach's ferocious demeanor on the football field, to see him lead a Friday night Boy Scout meeting, usually with a few dads present, we warmed to him. We wanted the behemoth we knew on the gridiron to invest his attention on us when we wore a different uniform, one with arm patches, copper buckles, and neckerchiefs.

Why Coach favored Frank Roberts over the rest of us, I don't know. Scrawny and short, he expelled a quiet demeanor and monotone voice. Or maybe it was the confident way he carried himself, with a refinement that I, with my heavy bulk and loud voice, envied. A straight-A student, Frank took it for granted when handed back a paper or test that he had aced it, whereas I feared opening the folded theme to find a red circled C- or worse, and on exams, a possible "Do Over."

I first witnessed Coach's affinity for Frank when our troop held an overnight in the kindergarten rooms at the elementary school. That night we played basketball in the gym, swung on leather-bound rings, whipped rubber balls back and forth at each other in bombard (today's "dodgeball"), and played indoor baseball.

Next morning, when waking up, I saw Frank lying alongside Coach in his sleeping bag. I wondered why Coach had picked Frank and not, well, me. Why was Frank getting all the affection? Frank now shared something with Coach that I did not, leaving me distraught and miserable.

That morning's yearning for an adult's attentiveness would continue until the day I wakened to the knowledge that an invitation for closeness and seclusion with an adult did not necessarily mean tenderness and affection.

Only once did Coach invite me into his domain. I don't remember where or when, only that he was handing out visits like Tootsie Roll Pops, calling us over one after another. When he finally recognized *me*, called *my* name, how grateful I was to be graced and accepted by him! Resting prone beside that massive bulk, assured that he found me worthy to enter his fold and now counted as one of his acolytes, I relaxed, knowing I now co-existed with Frank in Coach's coterie.

There was no penetration and no masturbation. At least I remember none. If anything, he might have run a hand over my body, but I don't remember where, or for how long. I will not make up what I cannot specify. I can testify, however, my pleasure — not physical that I remember — at the honor of being received. How kind. How generous. How gracious.

So why write about it now, 60 years later? Why when she asks what I've been writing this morning do I finally divulge the stories about Coach to my wife after 42 years of marriage? Catharsis? A need to confess something I was never guilty of?

Although convinced I did not encounter Coach's penis when tucked in his sleeping bag, I did encounter it once: erect and hard and straight as a circular ivory grave marker. Its size staggered my 12-year-old's imagination. "I could have one of *those* one day?" I surely mused, as much elated as terrified, because, at the time, I wondered what he was doing with it out.

The obelisk appeared during a troop road trip to Niagara Falls and New York City. We'd left the Midwest behind, now *putt-putt-putting* along a highway in Coach's Volkswagen Microbus. My turn to ride shotgun, I gloried in sitting near the big man while the raucous idiots in the middle seat were standing up, their faces and upper torsos stretched out the open sunroof, bucking the 60-mile-per-hour speed, laughing and shouting at the passing cars and trucks.

I suppose it was the dearth of traffic that prompted Coach to drive with one hand and with the other unzip his pants and flip out his penis. To us it must have seemed a testament of inviolable proof of manhood required to lead us boys into our future lives of Men of the World. What more could we ask for than his sharing and baring his dick, his prick, his cock, all those delightfully outrageous words our parents forbid us to utter, much less inquire about? Not only had an adult displayed one, but wait… he wanted us to *touch* it?

Even with three older brothers, I had no idea what a man should do, or want to do, with the mushroom-domed dowel posted beside me. I feared and hoped in equal amounts that my sexual education was about to commence. The horror! The grandeur!

But here's where I admit a confusion of memory. *Because* I was in the front seat, I would have been the nearest to the *objet d'art*, and therefore the most obvious boy to be asked, to be invited to pull him off. And maybe I did. I can't deny the possibility, because my younger self's desire to please, my need to let the scoutmaster know I could follow directions, and my weakness in resisting compliance to fulfill an adult's request all make the prospect plausible.

That I don't remember grabbing his member and jerking him off isn't proof that it didn't happen. Whether or not he ejaculated I cannot recall. I would imagine so; if not, why start the project? But I am blocked; my mind refuses to go there.

Looking back, what amazes me is what Coach knew what I, what we, did not know. He began to lecture us on methodology, all the while giving hand-on specificity. Without seatbelts, all attention inside the minivan was given to the demonstration, all eyes peering at the model on display.

There is no good ending to this narrative. By the time we learned about sex abuse and pedophilia, we'd gone on to lives too crowded to take the time to narc on the man whose outing would mean outing ourselves. It would mean bringing each of Coach's victims, boys by then men who may not want such a public declaration. Did we want to admit to such gullibility? Did we want people to laugh at our naivete?

Did we want our scoutmaster and coach to go to prison?

When his name came up at our class's anniversaries, ironically, it was usually the women who late in the evening, after a few drinks, would say, "Hey, what about that coach who…." One of us would say vaguely, "Yeah, he was weird," and stories never got told. It was too soon. It was always too soon.

So why write about it now, 60 years later? Why when she asks what I've been writing this morning do I finally divulge the stories about Coach to my wife after 42 years of marriage? Catharsis? A need to confess something I was never guilty of? A way to relieve subdued anger and confusion caused by a man whom we thought we could trust and from whom we thought we needed love?

Maybe. Or maybe now is time to reflect on those early years when I believed a man was worth believing in, even after he tore into me and left me stunned, damaged, and grounded. A time when the complexities and nuances of love and lust existed only in comics and magazines I snuck under the covers at night, not in the real world. Never in the real world. Because if they did exist in the world beyond puberty, it would mean someday having to engage them like they really existed.

Richard Holinger's books include *Kangaroo Rabbits* and *Galvanized Fences*, humorous essays, and *North of Crivitz*, poetry of the rural Upper Midwest. His prose and verse have appeared in *Southern Review, Witness, ACM, Cimarron Review, Boulevard,* and garnered four Pushcart Prize nominations. "Not Everybody's Nice" won the 2012 Split Oak Press Flash Prose Contest, and his "Thread" essay was designated a Notable in *Best American Essays, 2018*. His degrees include a PhD in creative writing from University of Illinois Chicago. He taught English in university, community college, and secondary school settings for over 40 years. Holinger lives west of Chicago far enough to see woods and foxes out his desk window.

Essay

Anything Unusual?

Carol W. Runyan

One warm spring afternoon in 1963 I was unable to find a playing partner, so I signed in at the clubhouse and ventured out alone carrying my yellow canvas bag aiming for nine holes before dinner. I had gotten my first set of golf clubs for Christmas the year before at age 12. At the time I had opened the package under the tree, hid my disappointment from my mother who clearly was excited to be giving the gift. She had been an avid golfer as a young woman and was eager to teach me and my brother how to play. I had not thought about learning to play golf and, ashamedly, did not find the gift exciting.

I was just starting puberty and proud that I had finally developed enough to wear my first training bra, like the other girls. Unlike other girls, I was not interested in spending my time after school talking about clothes, hairstyles, or giggling about dreamy TV stars or the gawky boys in our class. Instead, I headed to the golf course as often as possible.

Our small quiet village in central Ohio had a lush green course nestled amidst rolling hills on the edge of town. It bordered the high school football field on one side and was surrounded on the other sides by green pastures and hillsides thick with forests. The course buzzed on weekends, but was rarely crowded late in the day on weekdays.

Though boys my age paid little attention to me at school, I enjoyed the easygoing relationships with older high school boys on the golf course, some of them friends of my brother. Often I just played with whomever was around — working men who came for a quick round after work or several grandfatherly types who were especially friendly to us kids, coaching us a bit while we played. When no one else was around, I would play alone, sometimes hitting two balls for practice, scoring each ball's round as if two different players were competing. I never thought about safety. Our town in that era was devoid of the kinds of crimes that we watched unfold in weekly episodes of *Perry Mason*.

This particular late afternoon, the course was practically empty. I started off on the first hole across the swift creek that all too often swallowed my errant balls. This time, though, I drove my ball easily across and up near the green, then set off with my cleats clicking across the wooden bridge.

Enveloped in the fresh, sweet scent of the cut fairways and the gradual cooling as the sun got lower in the sky, sliding just above the hills to the west, I played the first four holes. They were mostly straight, with fairways separated only by a few trees, sandtraps, and low rough. The fifth hole was more challenging, along the side of a hill. Balls struck too far to the right might land among the oaks or nestle behind a large pine tree that guarded the right side of the green. Too far left and down the slope meant tall, thick grass, not a good line of sight to the flag, and a steep climb back up to reach the green. Going straight required some finesse to miss an ominous sandtrap with a deep lip in the front of the green.

I was always pleased to reach the sixth hole, having completed the difficult number five. Six was a short par three in the farthest corner of the course up the slope behind the fifth green. This 130-yard par three was short enough I could reach the green with my drive, giving me a sense of accomplishment in making par and maybe even a chance for a birdie. It wasn't an easy hole, though, with a steep dropoff to the right into the rocky wooded hillside that bordered number five. Thickets of prickly bushes lined the left side along a barbed wire fence separating the course from a cow pasture. Someone had constructed a sort of ladder to allow players to scale the fence to retrieve hooked balls. The fence posts were wobbly, though, allowing cows to slip through occasionally and wander onto the course. My mother had always tried to quell my fears of various types of critters with "they're more scared of you than you are of them." But, I was not completely convinced when it came to cows.

Despite the prospect of meeting cows, the sixth and seventh holes were my favorites. The seventh was magical. The fairway cut through thick woods where I could imagine I was a pioneer girl exploring new terrain, just like stories of my favorite author, Laura Ingalls Wilder. I loved hearing the birds and squirrels gently rustling fallen leaves, interrupted only by the far away sound of the college chimes across town, signalling the change of the hour.

On this day, as I climbed up a short, steep hill to get to the sixth tee, I savoured the warm sunshine and the view out over the holes below. I saw no other players. Thankfully, no cows were in view either. I pulled out my five iron, stuck my tee in the ground, and took several practice swings. Looking up, I spotted a scruffy man with unkempt hair emerge from the woods below. He wore gray pants and matching shirt, similar to what the janitors at my school wore. But, unlike the neatly dressed janitors, his clothes were rumpled and stained. I didn't recall having seen him before, though it was not unusual for people to comb the edges of the fairways and woods looking for lost balls they could re-sell to passing golfers. I had played with numerous men who stopped, exchanged pleasantries with these ball-gatherers, and paid a dollar or two for several balls.

After my ball landed on the left edge of the green and I slid my club back into my bag, the man in grey lay down on his side, lounging at the right edge of the green looking toward where my ball had landed. That seemed odd, but I continued toward the green. He didn't move. I was puzzled. When I got to the green, I noticed that his pants were unzipped and his genitals were in full view, dangling through the opening. Our family was pretty relaxed about nudity so seeing a man's penis was not, in itself, novel or shocking. I had caught glimpses of my father at various times while he was dressing. But, this scene surely did strike me as unusual.

The man didn't speak or move as I approached my ball. He just watched as I put my bag down on the other side of the small green and pulled out my putter. I nodded, trying to ignore what he was showing, and said "hello" as if this was a perfectly normal encounter. I knew it wasn't. Then I walked quickly to the next tee hoping to move on and away from him. While he had not done anything threatening and was not as scary as the cows I worried about encountering, I found his behavior unsettling.

He followed me the short distance to the seventh tee, standing back while I teed off. I went ahead and smacked the best drive I could, remaining in "normal" mode. As I stepped off the tee toward where my ball had landed in the fairway some 150 yards ahead, he offered to carry my bag. I politely replied, "no thanks." My pulse quickened as I was starting to get more uncomfortable, but I still was not particularly frightened even though I knew we were in the most remote location on the course out of earshot of anyone.

As I started down the fairway, my rumpled follower trailed about ten feet behind. Gradually, he edged closer and closer as his grubby hands pulled a handful of golf balls from his pants pocket. He moved close and dropped them into the top of my bag. As they rattled to the bottom, I politely thanked him. At this point, I realized that something didn't feel quite right and instinctively decided it was time to take action.

I explained how he offered to carry my bag, followed me, and gave me golf balls and how I had told him that my dad was waiting. I explained all the details — except one.

Without deliberation, I looked quickly at the Timex on my wrist and sharply declared a falsehood, "Oh my god, I'm late and my dad is waiting on the next tee."

I picked up the ball I had hit and started to move toward the green as fast as I could while carrying a full bag of clubs with a handful of extra balls jangling inside. I glanced back and noticed the man disappear into the woods. My breathing finally slowed as I reached the eighth tee. Often I lingered on that tee high atop the course enjoying the view. This time I teed off hastily, played just one ball, and rapidly headed down the winding path to the fairway below, relieved by the sight of the clubhouse about 400 yards ahead.

I was pleased with my quick thinking in saying that my dad was nearby when, in fact, he was probably still in his office at the college atop another hill across town. I played the final two holes. Then, once back at the clubhouse, I calmly called my mother as planned, telling her I was ready for a ride home in time for supper.

As I look back more than half a century later, I am amazed by the calm that my naivete enabled. At the same time, I am horrified about what could have happened. I had been taught to be cautious and not to accept rides from strangers and had applied that directive a few years earlier when a man offered me a ride to school. He was our family doctor who had made housecalls multiple times to care for my tonsilitis, but I didn't recognize him in his car and refused the ride. He called my parents to report the incident, worried that I might be afraid, and my parents praised me for not getting in the car when I was unsure. I also remember my dad, a psychologist, reflecting on how fearless my mother had been when forced to confront psychotic men during the time they they both worked in a psychiatric hospital. Perhaps that story echoed in my brain unconsciously during this golf course event, bolstering my courage.

If I told my parents right away about the encounter, I certainly did not reveal the part about the man exposing himself. In fact, it was not until I was an adult that I told anyone about that.

But, I must have said something about the encounter to my golfing friends at school because a day or two later, a local police officer phoned our house in the evening just after I had gotten into bed. My parents got me up to come to the phone. They sat nearby while I, in my pajamas, listened as the officer explained that a man, perhaps the same one, had that day grabbed one of my two girl friends while they were playing in this same remote part of the course.

He asked me to describe the man I had seen. Tightly grasping the phone, I slowly told of the grubby gray clothes he was wearing and his uncombed light brown hair. I explained how he offered to carry my bag, followed me, and gave me golf balls and how I had told him that my dad was waiting. I explained all the details — except one.

The officer probed further, "Was there anything unusual about him?"

"No," I said, hesitantly.

He tried again, gently, "Is there was anything else you can tell me about him that might have been unusual."

Quietly, "No."

I knew that what I had seen was not usual, but I did not know the terminology to use to explain how he had exposed himself without having to name the body parts I had seen — something way too embarrassing to talk about with a male officer on the phone. More troubling than the description I was hiding was the fact I was not telling the whole truth. I had been taught to always be honest. But, embarrassment had overshadowed my moral code.

As I became a health professional, I learned about sexual assault and felt fortunate that my encounter, though technically counted as an assault, was minor and left no scars. I also have learned how important good interviewing techniques are in getting children to reveal accurate information about the circumstances of traumatic events.

After the event, I continued to play golf as often as I could but my parents encouraged me to play with others and asked me after each round about my playing partners. I could sense their concern, particularly on days I had stayed on the course as dusk descended. Though I still sometimes played alone, I was more vigilant about where I was on the course, keeping a watchful eye for more than wandering bovines.

I recently reconnected with one of the friends who experienced the assault in the days after my encounter. She revealed how scared she had been going to the police station to identify the assailant and how angry she now was that her mother had implied that the other girl who had been grabbed had somehow brought on the attack by her choice of clothes. She also revealed that the experience led her to quit playing golf entirely. In different ways, we each had lost some innocence that week.

In reality, the event was far more traumatic when I reflected on it as an adult than it was at the time. At the time, I had derived some sense of power at having managed the immediate situation successfully; plus, for me nothing bad had happened. It was just weird. Reflecting as an adult, I am struck that both my friend and I recall, now more than five decades later, clear details of our experiences. We are well aware that our "#metoo" experiences could have unfolded in much different ways.

A few days after the incident, the officer called again. This time, he reported that they had caught a man who confessed to grabbing my friend. He reported, chillingly, that the man had declared, "I always let them go when they scream."

Carol W. Runyan is a mostly retired public health professor who has taught at University of North Carolina Gillings School of Global Public Health and at the Colorado School of Public Health with a specialization in injury and violence prevention. She is an avid golfer who has won a few local tournaments over the years and hopes to someday shoot her age. She lives in North Carolina with her husband and spends her time teaching public health, reading, and writing when not swinging a club.

Rugby History

A Long Road Home: Getting There From Here

Lance Mason

Sport creates legends, living icons woven into the fabric of our lives, our societies, heroes who endure in history: Jim Thorpe, Lou Gehrig, Jackie Robinson, Wilma Rudolph, Sandy Koufax, Colin Kaepernick. A hero among heroes, Muhammad Ali's magnetism impacted a wider world, a world that had embraced Fanny Blankers-Koen and Emil Zátopek, Pelé and Peter Snell, and later Navratilova and Nadal, all of whom stood, or stand, for issues larger than themselves.

Public figures have often argued against mixing politics and sports, while reality shows that the neural synapses that fire in the execution of, and admiration of, athletic feats will scatter their sparks into the roiled conflicts of history — Jesse Owens vs. Adolf Hitler, Branch Rickey vs. Major League Baseball, the '68 Mexico Games, Megan Rapinoe and Lebron James vs. the Politics of Trump. Yet there was another conflict, another sporting war, largely unknown in the United States, which began small but became one of the great legacies to justice of the 20th century.

In pre-Victorian England, c. 1823, a new sport sprang to life at Rugby School, Warwickshire. After a slow start in its home country, the game began to flourish, gradually taken up in British enclaves around the globe. By the 1850s, as well as thriving in the British Armed Forces, rugby football became identified with the upper classes and their schools. This image, however, did not hold in all corners of the Empire.

Though distant from the motherland and each other, New Zealand and South Africa did share certain traits. Both were governed under British law, patterned their school systems after Britain's, and enjoyed farming as a major strut in their economies. And, in both countries, rugby spread like a contagious rash. Yet, unlike Britain and its other colonies, the two fledgling nations drew their players from the common walks of life — farmers, teachers, police, tradesmen, dentists, doctors, cobblers.

In New Zealand, the rash would become a vigorous passion, spreading far and deep, with the town of Nelson hosting the country's first rugby match in 1870. By 1905, NZ had sent a ship-borne team to tour Europe, posting a record of 34-1-0, with "test match" victories over the national teams of England, Ireland, Scotland, and France. An English journalist christened the exotic visitors the All Blacks (that color wool being the least costly for a traveling band on a budget to produce back home). Today in New Zealand that team is remembered as The Originals. In 1925 the All Blacks would return to Europe in an unbeaten 32-0 run against nations whose total populations were nearly 100 times New Zealand's. Every Kiwi school kid knows them as The Invincibles.

Yet this was only half the story.

Prior to WW I, South Africa had also dominated the teams of Britain. NZ's 1928 All Blacks played a 22-match tour through South Africa, winning most, but managing only two wins out of four national tests against SA's Springboks. These early NZ-SA contests foretold what would become the greatest rivalry in rugby history, and a century of these intense battles would one day write quite another history. For rugby's profile in these two regions had long ago diverged: In New Zealand, indigenous players and *pākehā* (ethnic Europeans) were integrated from the start, but segregated in South Africa.

Rugby's fan numbers are quite small compared to soccer's and other sports, so its role in geopolitics registers little in the media. Hence, few globally could have grasped the enormous influence New Zealand would hold in post-WW II South Africa. In counterpoint, Apartheid, set in law from 1949, with its odious, race-based facism, was soon to face serious confrontations.

Facing mounting global pressure to integrate its sports, a stubborn South Africa resisted, quitting the Commonwealth in 1961. Banishment from international soccer soon followed. South Africa's whites-only teams were banned from 1964's Tokyo Summer Games and, for a decade, international track-and-field haggled, then axed SA in 1971. Their chess team met the same fate when — yes — Albania refused to play them. Cricket sanctions began in the 1960s and were almost total within 10 years.

However, in the context of this time and place, the core sporting identity for white residents in South Africa was rugby football, orders of magnitude greater than all the rest. The force of rugby's social and political role in White South Africa couldn't be overstated, and this was a connection closely shared with New Zealand, the two maintaining rugby contact throughout these turbulent years. When all the sporting world was saying, "Don't let the door hit you in the ass," the New Zealand Rugby Football Union (NZRFU) stood by South Africa, continuing to play them. This meant everything to White South Africa and their beloved rugby. But that would change.

For decades, the NZRFU had indulged South Africa's racist policies, which included barring Māori from playing on NZ teams in South Africa. In 1960 the first wrinkle accompanied this complicity, when a "No Māori – No Tour" petition was signed by 160,000 Kiwis, most of them young adults with an eye for change. While an all-*pākehā* team went to South Africa that year, it would be NZ's last. The Springboks toured New Zealand in 1965 with little conflict, even against Māori teams. But the racism persisted. A Kiwi telegrapher saved this dispatch from one South African sportswriter to his paper at home:

> BAD ENOUGH HAVING TO PLAY OFFICIALLY DESIGNATED NEW ZEALAND NATIVES, BUT SPECTACLE THOUSANDS EUROPEANS FRANTICALLY CHEERING ON BAND OF COLOURED MEN TO DEFEAT MEMBERS OF OWN RACE WAS TOO MUCH FOR SPRINGBOKS WHO FRANKLY DISGUSTED.

Meanwhile, segments of NZ's rugby community were indeed awakening. The All Blacks canceled a 1967 SA tour and rerouted to Europe. Then NZ refused to exclude Māori and Pacific Island players from a 1970 South Africa tour. SA's answer: Any non-whites must accept "honorary white citizenship." Otherwise, no referees or doctors would attend the matches. NZ did bring their *Pasifika* players, but cooperated with the masquerade.

The showdown — the events that would spell an end to Apartheid — began in 1976, but had its antecedents. Anti-Springbok protests in Australia had spawned serious violence in 1971, and NZ axed an incoming 1973 SA tour on advice from NZ Police of similar risks. Yet in 1976, before that year's Montréal Olympics, the All Blacks toured South Africa once again — with their "honorary white citizens." The rugby results were unremarkable; the political results were not. More than 20 African nations demanded New Zealand be banned from both the Olympics and the IOC. Both proposals failed, and those nations walked out of the Montréal Games.

Yes, Kiwis are fierce sports competitors, but in person are unfailingly hospitable and gracious. Now their athletes and citizens had been globally shamed, ridiculed internationally because of rugby, something for which they have enormous pride and affection. Thus, a latent infection against South Africa began to fester in NZ, and Kiwi groups like HART (Halt All Racist Tours) renewed the fight against Apartheid. Then, in 1977, by signing the Gleneagles Agreement, the Commonwealth of Nations agreed to end all sporting contact with South Africa.

For years afterward, Bishop Desmond Tutu spoke frankly how Kiwis demonstrating against the Springboks in the streets of Auckland spelled the end of Apartheid.

Still, despite years of disrespect inflicted on Māori by SA, despite the Australian riots of 1971 and the NZ warnings of 1973, despite the ridicule NZ suffered in Montréal, and despite Gleneagles, the NZRFU and Prime Minister Rob Muldoon approved, in 1980, a new Springboks' tour to New Zealand. (Under "tone deaf c. 1980," the *Oxford English Dictionary* has a photo of Robert Muldoon.)

What followed was, in precise journalistic terms, a cluster f*ck. From the Springboks' arrival in July 1981, anti-Apartheid riots became the order of the day in NZ. Those who'd signed the *No Māori-No Tour* petitions in 1960, now mature adults and parents, supported the long-held credo, "Segregation has no place in NZ." Protesters occupied stadiums, tore down fences, battled with police, and flour-bombed rugby matches from the air. Matches that should have sold out were played to empty stadiums, others canceled for fear of violence.

In South Africa, the reactions to the New Zealand broadcasts were earth-shaking. Their bond with NZ was their anchor to world recognition in sport, in life. Yet watching "the Springbok Riots" made them sincerely appalled, even frightened. What had their world come to when the police could not, would not stop people — and white people, at that — protesting against the traditions they held dear, a dogma that declared that rugby was all that mattered? Why worry about the insignificant sports like soccer and track and cricket when the Springboks and All Blacks were *brothers in rugby*? For decades, SA's fans had listened on the "wireless" across 10,000 miles of ocean as two sweating Goliaths battled it out on the high veldt of the Transvaal or verdant fields in the Antipodes. This was the world's toughest sport, and no other nation could carry South Africa's or New Zealand's jockstrap. Now that reality was being shattered, crushed by a hammer-blow from their closest allies.

To Bishop Desmond Tutu, however, and his anti-apartheid allies, these scenes were heaven on earth, a gift from the gods. For years afterward, Tutu spoke frankly how Kiwis demonstrating against the Springboks in the streets of Auckland spelt the end of Apartheid. "When South African rugby was treated as a pariah by its greatest rival, that really shook them." Tutu knew that White South Africa would have to choose between Apartheid and rugby. "For us, this was a shot in the arm."

South Africa would be cut off from rugby contact with New Zealand for the next 11 years. In 1987, the Springboks were banned from the first Rugby World Cup. New Zealand hosted, and won the tournament. For South Africa, this was unendurable.

It took some time, but change was coming.

As SA languished in rugby prison, Nelson Mandela lived in a true prison, on Robben Island. There, in a stone-and-concrete cell, for 18 years he slept on a mat, sat on a stool, and shat in a bucket — a life more humane than that inflicted on many of his people. Mandela, though, had spent a further nine years in other prisons — 27 years in pursuit of freedom:

> *I have dedicated myself to the struggle of the African people, fought against white domination, and fought against black domination. I have cherished the ideal of a democratic and free society in which all persons live together in harmony and with equal opportunities. It is an ideal which I hope to live for and to achieve. But if it needs be, it is an ideal for which I am prepared to die.*

After the All Blacks' R.W.C. victory, discussions began in South Africa for Mandela's release, eventually granted in 1990. While the Springboks were again banned from the World Cup in 1991, the All Blacks returned to SA in 1992, defeating the Springboks in Johannesburg. A South African club team was invited that year to an important tournament in Hong Kong. Two years later, with Mr. Mandela as South Africa's new President, the Springboks played a 14-match tour of NZ, finishing 10-2-1, defeated by the All Blacks in two of three national team matches.

Then the dam broke — South Africa was invited to host the 1995 Rugby World Cup.

After centuries of white domination and decades of Apartheid, President Nelson Mandela[1], trying to heal the wounds, called on his people, white and black, to support "their boys." All of South Africa rallied to the cause. After the elimination rounds, 16 countries competed at venues across SA. The Springboks won the Final, defeating the All Blacks 12-9 in overtime.

Rugby today in South Africa is an integrated sport. Gentlemen of Color on the Springboks have become heroes to Boys of Color across the land. In 2019, Siyamthanda Kolisi captained the Springboks, the first Black skipper in the long list of names stamped in gold in the iconography of South African Rugby. Kolisi led the 'Boks to victory in 2019's Rugby World Cup, South Africa's third title — a number shared only with, of course, New Zealand. Justice is sweet, sayeth the Rugby Gods.

In truth, dogged forces in New Zealand opposed the 1981 Springbok Riots, opposed change. For years, some Kiwis didn't want that fight. But you can't

---

[1] Is it a minor coincidence that Mr. Mandela's first name matches that of the first town in which rugby was played in New Zealand?

stop justice in a just nation, in a just society. You can't stop the momentum of honest, courageous people doing the right thing. How long would Apartheid have endured without New Zealand's reversal from complicity to unbridled opposition? No one can say. But a person, a team, or a nation, with courage and commitment to a goal, will rise up and conquer what can seem like an indivisible monolith. What these events showed is that the world's community of nations will not accept race-based discrimination as a social construct.

Lance Mason, who was raised in rural California, worked blue-collar jobs before studying at University of California at Santa Barbara, Loyola (BSc), and UCLA (doctorate). He has held several teaching posts in the United States, New Zealand, and Brazil, has presented at UCSB's College of Creative Studies, and won a scholarship to the VCFA 2016 Postgraduate Writers Conference. His writing has appeared in a variety of literary journals, magazines, and professional journals, winning numerous awards as well as selection for *The Best Travel Writing, Volume 11* (2016). A veteran *Sport Literate* essayist, Mason has published essays within these pages since 2016.

Essay Contest Winner

The Cardinal, the Cops, and the Say-Hey Kid

Sydney Lea

It gets stranger and stranger as I knock on eighty's door, the way some random thing can summon a skein of apparently unrelated memories, though in some cases it feels more like an explosion than a summons.

A cardinal flew into one of our windows a few mornings ago. We heard the pop against the glass and went to inspect. There the lovely bird lay on new-fallen snow, the very emblem of conspicuous. I watched as my wife went out and picked up his corpse. Dislodged feathers lifted in the January wind, and blood dotted the whited ground in an almost perfect circle around the body.

I was swiftly, unaccountably, jarringly swept back seven decades.

No winter day then, but one in June of 1951. I'd been tingling with excitement since the night before, because my father was taking me to my first major league baseball game. We'd be going courtesy of some friend I didn't know, a season ticketholder. Dad assured me this meant our spot in the stands would be better than almost anyone's. He also told me we'd see a rookie who, he predicted, would become a once-in-a-lifetime player. When I asked this star's name, he said, "You'll find out soon enough."

I was intrigued. I mean, Dad had seen Babe Ruth play in his time! I didn't yet know much about the major leagues, but everyone — man, woman, fan, non-fan, kids big and little, everyone! — recognized the illustrious Bambino's name. Would this fellow outshine the Babe? Looking back, I think my father meant once in my lifetime.

He'd be right, as he so often was, bless him. But I get ahead of myself.

All the while Dad and I made our way to our gate at old Connie Mack Stadium, I vainly sought to disengage my hand from his. I wanted to look like more than a youngster. Five times a parent and seven a grandparent since then, I now completely understand his worry that I might get lost among the milling pedestrians.

We were suddenly halted by a clot of them, some cheering as if they were already at the game. I could see nothing but a mass of bodies, but my tall dad observed what was going on, or rather had gone on. His grip got harder, painfully so, as he dragged me across the street and away from the gawkers.

Despite his strategy, it was from the far side of that small crowd that I could turn and see a black man lying stone-still on the sidewalk, his blood bright against the gray of its concrete. Two cops, one short and pot-bellied, the other tall and slim as a wand, loomed over him, each fondling a night stick and each, it appeared, half-smiling. The fallen man's face, however improbably, looked as peaceful as a sleeping person's. The whole scene completely bewildered and, to euphemize, unsettled me; it has also stayed with me since, even though my look at it was so fleeting.

I importuned my father: "What happened? What did that guy do?" He answered tersely: "I can't say, son. Could be anything." Then, his face showing an expression I'd never seen in all my brief time on earth, he added, "or nothing."

"But why," I asked, "would they beat him up for nothing?" Dad just pulled me along even faster.

"Why?" I insisted. Silence.

A whole lot makes grim sense to me now that didn't when I was so young and guileless. The second great war had ended a mere six years before, and while this was an eternity to a small child, it was an eyeblink to my father, who had commanded a company of so-called Colored Troops during that epical conflict. Though probably eight out of 10 Americans today don't realize as much, it was not until 1948 that President Truman desegregated U.S. armed forces by executive order.

My father rarely mentioned his time in military service, and at such rare moments as he did, it was generally to tell us some funny anecdote. It was therefore my mother who much later told a story that was anything but amusing, and that actually accounted for my being born in Pennsylvania.

Before their transfer to Wales a year and some later and ultimately to Normandy, my dad's unit, all African-American save the commissioned officers, had been stationed in Gadsden, Alabama, the very heart of Jim Crow Dixie. It was my father's conviction, she said, and local customs be damned, that if he wanted to invite one or more of his soldiers into his Gadsden house, well, he would simply do it. Local customs, as it turned out, involved burning a cross on the lawn of any man who entertained such an unacceptable notion.

All but immediately after that incident, my mother chose to flee north to have her firstborn, me. The night before she took the northbound train, however, she woke her husband in the wee hours, convinced she'd heard the sound of a human being in torment outside. Dad, having circled the base with a flashlight and spoken to a sentry, concluded she'd imagined the noise, rattled as she was by the cross-burning. He went back to sleep. She didn't.

It was about a decade later, three years after Jackie Robinson broke the color barrier in major league baseball — on that Sunday afternoon in June, we finally arrived at our entry into Connie Mack Stadium. A short, rotund man, chewing a dead cigar, took our tickets and, annoyingly, tousled my hair. We were in.

I have a number of stunning memories from that day, the first of which I have described. Others, thank God, are for the most part less grotesque than that one. I can still distinctly picture what I beheld once we emerged from the concrete tunnel to the ballfield: an awesome expanse of green. I remember it literally made me catch my breath. I thought it almost impossible that anyone would besmirch that huge, pristine span of grass by playing a game on it. But for all of that, there were busy human figures out there.

Once we'd found our seats, perhaps five rows back from the home team Phillies' dugout, my father whispered: "That's a guy to watch." He pointed to a man, notable as one of three black Giants, who was shagging fungo flies in center field. He did not say that Giant was the guy to watch, just a guy.

"Why watch him?" I asked. Was that man the star Dad had hinted at? I supposed so but wasn't quite sure.

"Why him?" I repeated.

"You'll see," he replied.

I was curious, to be sure, but also sufficiently entranced by the vista that I didn't even feel impatient for play to begin. But by and by, of course, the players did come off the field and into their dugouts until the P.A. announcer read off the names of the starters for both teams. As the Giants players were introduced and stepped out to face the crowd, the hometown fans booed. That seemed understandable; these were our opponents, after all. But I got confused when, at the words Willie Mays, the jeering got notably louder.

I looked over at my father, who shook his head, if just perceptibly.

Mays batted third in the order. After both preceding hitters grounded out, he sent a single over the second base bag. The hit didn't seem especially impressive. But when the cleanup man stepped into the box — as with so many on both sides, I don't recall his name — Willie took what looked like a perilous lead off first. I do remember that Russ Myer pitched for the Phillies that afternoon, and that three times he tried a pickoff, Willie scooting back to the bag without the slightest difficulty.

On Myer's first delivery home, however, Mays lit out, slid into the second-base bag yards ahead of catcher Andy Seminick's throw, and popped to his feet with a broad smile on his face. Even at nine, I could somehow discern glee in this man's expression, not mockery. He was having fun! Willie took an equally daring lead toward third, but the Giants' cleanup hitter popped harmlessly to the first baseman and the top half of that first inning was over.

In 1965, I watched TV footage from the state my mother had fled when she was eight months pregnant, the very one in which the great Willie Mays was born. Combat-geared, white officers, with their dogs, their clubs, and their hoses, were attacking peaceful demonstrators as they crossed a bridge in Selma.

"Boy, he's fast," I remarked. My father only smiled.

The Phillies' first batter walked, but the two following were uneventfully retired. Then Del Ennis scorched a line drive, and a loud cheer erupted all around us — until the center fielder chased it down, almost casually snaring the potential hit with one hand. Mays's put-out induced an eerie quiet from the stands.

In Mays's second at-bat, I watched his homer clear the opposite field wall, and in one of the later innings, I saw him lay down a perfect sacrifice bunt. Clearly, he could do about anything he wanted.

What I particularly recall but can't quite render in words is that, despite his very recent arrival to the big leagues, whenever this player came to the plate or stood on base or made for a fly ball, the atmosphere in the stadium was instantly, and as I say indescribably, changed, anticipation hanging in the air as thick as the cigar and cigarette smoke all around us. Despite the occasional vile shout from Phillies fans, including the unforgivable N-word, there was just something irrepressible about this player's manner. No amount of boorishness could ever quash it, I felt sure.

I have some fancy terms in my old age that I did not command then, ones like dynamism, verve, elan. Any and all of them would have applied to this amazing athlete, who, in the bottom of the ninth, threw a strike to the plate from deep left center to nab a potentially tying baserunner and end the contest into the bargain.

The game over, we stood to exit the park. I looked up at my father, ready to state the obvious, that here was a person whose capacities and character were unmatched by any I'd ever witnessed.

I didn't get the chance. Seeing my expression, he simply said, "I told you... and he'll be getting even better."

In the later years of this demigod's 22 in the majors, it would pain me to watch him on television. Most of his supernal skills evaporated, he now and then actually bumbled around in the outfield at Shea. In my late twenties by then, I would literally close my eyes when he took a feeble swing at a breaking ball or failed to chase down a fly or stood a mere foot or two off first if he did happen to get there. I didn't want to know him after his prime, didn't want to blemish that earliest of sporting memories. To this day wish I hadn't.

During that game in 1951, I'd been more or less distracted from the sight of the man the cops had knocked to the ground, but I think I know now why my father led us back to the parking lot by a circuitous route. No doubt the police were gone — who knew what had happened to their victim? — so I'd bet he worried some bloodstains might remain on street or sidewalk. I never asked.

I skip ahead to another Sunday, this one in 1965. I was a year out of college and, like so many, I watched TV footage from the state my mother had fled when she was eight months pregnant, the very one in which the great Willie Mays was born. Combat-geared, white officers, with their dogs, their clubs, and their hoses, were attacking peaceful demonstrators as they crossed a bridge in Selma. Bodies lay inert on the pavement as the phalanx of police made its brutal way through the throng.

I called home that evening from the apartment I shared with two friends not far from the stadium, then in its 56th year of existence. I don't remember what I said to Dad by way of expressing my horror, but I vividly remember what he said just before we finished our conversation.

"I won't live to see it, but you'll see a black president of the United States."

The whole notion was so unfathomably and uncharacteristically asinine that I didn't even respond.

And yet my father turned out to be right on all counts: in 1966, the very next year, he'd drop dead, breaking my heart — and I would live to see Barack Obama serve two terms as America's chief executive.

If only that interlude could have changed my country as much as millions of us hoped.

I recall something else from my June afternoon in 1951, something very odd indeed, given all that transpired that day. Brief as my glimpse of the beaten man had been, as we rode home in silence, I remember thinking that his face, unwrinkled and youthfully handsome, resembled the face of Willie Mays. This was not a matter of racial identity, not one of those abhorrent they-all-look-alike surmises. The supine man on the pavement did not remind me at all, say, of Willie's African-American teammates Monte Irvin and Hank Thompson. It just somehow struck me that the downed man, given far different circumstances, might break into a dynamic smile, full, yes, of verve and elan.

That notion puzzled the hell out of me, and I badly wanted to purge it from my mind — which would take a lot longer than I might have predicted. In fact, to this day I obviously haven't succeeded.

A few days ago, I felt deep, seemingly disproportionate sorrow as I held the dead cardinal in my hand. I hated to do it, but I stepped inside, lifted the top of our woodstove, and dropped in his brilliant body, which felt almost as light as air.

Sydney Lea is 2021 recipient of his home state Vermont's most prestigious artist's distinction: the Governor's Award for Excellence in the Arts. (Past winners include luminaries from Galway Kinnell to Bernard Malamud, Grace Paley, Rudolf Serkin, and many others.) A former Pulitzer finalist and winner of the Poets' Prize, he served as founding editor of *New England Review* and was Vermont's Poet Laureate from 2011 to 2015). He is the author of 23 books, the latest *Seen from All Sides: Lyric and Everyday Life*, essays (Green Writers Press, 2021). The mock-epic graphic poem, "The Exquisite Triumph of Wormboy" (Able Muse, 2020), was produced in collaboration with former Vermont Cartoonist Laureate James Kochalka. Four Way Books (NYC) published *Here*, poems, in late 2019.

Contest Judge

On Our Essay Winner
Virginia Ottley Craighill

My father took us to Braves games in the 1970s. We sat in the cheap, unshaded plastic seats, and the backside of my legs would get slick with sweat. Atlanta was hot, baseball was slow, and I don't remember whether we won or lost, but I knew we were there to see one player in particular: Hank Aaron, Hammering Hank, a Black man who transcended race in the racist South and became a hometown hero.

"The Cardinal, the Cops, and the Say-Hey Kid," Sydney Lea's essay about seeing Willie Mays play for the first time reminded me of those hot summer days in Atlanta. So did his description of the Black man lying in a pool of blood on the sidewalk outside the stadium. Mr. Lea recalls the memory of his childhood, juxtaposing the child's first vision of racial violence with the joy of seeing the athletic genius of Mays in early career.

Though set in Connie Mack stadium in 1951 and focused on Mays and his boundary-breaking career, the more nuanced story of Lea's father provides the emotional core. When his father took him to that game, he already knew the evils of racism and segregation, and as a former commander of an all-Black unit in World War II in Europe and Gadsden, Alabama, had fought against it.

Lea's essay moves from his childhood memory of watching the Giants play the Phillies that June day to stories of his father's life before Lea was born, to a memory of a conversation with his father centered around an historical moment in the Civil Rights movement. Even in the main narrative, Lea shows us that racial violence and tension existed outside, and inside, the stadium, and reveals his father's regret that his son has to witness it.

Horror and hope exist simultaneously in Lea's narrative. Despite all evidence to the contrary, both he and his father believe that there will be racial justice, both on the playing field and in the nation. The young Lea thinks of Mays, "Clearly, he could do anything he wanted," and his father tells him after witnessing the televised police brutality in Selma in 1965 that there will be a Black president.

Mays, as a Black man in 1951, could not "do anything he wanted," and though Barack Obama became the first Black president, as Lea's father predicted, Lea reminds us through his framing image of the cardinal that the racial violence and injustice has not ended.

Going through the Atlanta airport about 10 years ago, my husband saw Hank Aaron on the escalator above us. He wanted to stop Aaron and introduce our children to him, perhaps ask for an autograph. But there was something in Aaron's face, a hint of pain and of residual anger from a lifetime of struggle against racism. We left him alone.

Sydney Lea's essay subtly reveals the ways unquestioned and irrational racial hatred lead inevitably to violence, but also the ways an individual can choose to reject that perspective, no matter how ingrained it is in our society, and to teach others to do the same.

Virginia Ottley Craighill grew up in Atlanta, Georgia, and received her Ph.D. in English and Creative Writing from the University of Georgia. She has been teaching English at the University of the South in Sewanee, Tennessee since 2001, and lives in Sewanee. She has commentary on the letters of Tennessee Williams in the Winter 2018 issue of *The Sewanee Review* and had a chapter on Eudora Welty in the volume "Teaching the Works of Eudora Welty." Her poems have been published in *Gulf Coast*, *The Chattahoochee Review*, and *Kalliope*, among others. Her *Sport Literate* essay, "The Lost Cause," was anthologized in *Best American Sports Writing 2019*.

Poetry Contest Winner
Wrestling Lake Burn
Flavian Mark Lupinetti

One, I count, as the bus driver boards.
Two, the head coach, takes the seat behind Bussy.
Three through nineteen, the rest of the team save
Cimino, twenty, last in his double sweats,
who must sweat off two pounds by six p.m.
Twenty-one, me, the assistant coach.
We go to wrestle Lake Burn.
To Cimino, a senior, we defer as he starts his routine
running the aisle forward and back, absent of expression
while the other wrestlers play video games
on their smartphones and text their friends.

In my day all we did was talk.
Cimino does not talk, he runs.
He runs through the West Virginia sunset,
five o'clock this time of year,
while the pines fashion foggy coats
to wrap themselves against the night.

Armed Forces Career Day at school today.
The sergeant wore a natty uniform,
the kids' faces mirrored in his shoes.
He delivered his message, straight from the heart,
straight from the best advertising agencies,
focus-group tested, results guaranteed.
Plenty of enlistments or your money back.
Afterward at practice the kids still clutch brochures,
pens, stickers, and baseball caps with military logo.
Cimino has them, too.

Please don't let them take Cimino.
You just get closer to some kids than others.
You never know why.
Please don't let them take any of them.
But especially don't let them take Cimino.

Cimino strips naked before submitting to the Toledo scale.
Then steps on boldly. One twenty-six and a half.
Now he can eat a candy bar.
Now he can eat a warm orange.
The head coach warns him, not too much.
Enter the gym and smell the mat cleaner,
a fragrance that never fails to make my heart race.

Spectators fill the stands —
fill, a relative term in wrestling.
Seventy, eighty people, mostly Lake Burners,
mostly family and friends of our opponents.
A few from our place.
Cimino's pregnant girlfriend among them

Under the constellation Orion.
We leave the gym and board the bus.
One, two... twenty-one
At least eighteen asleep before we reach the highway.
I hope they finished their homework.
I hope they don't have exams tomorrow.
The gears protest when the bus lumbers up the hill
as if climbing a back road in Nepal
instead of West By God Virginia.
When we level off the diesel drone
makes me nod.
Halfway home I hear footsteps so familiar
that I need not peek to see who approaches.
He takes the empty seat to my left,
the sergeant's brochure in his hand.

Flavian Mark Lupinetti, a poet, fiction writer, cardiac surgeon, and former wrestling coach, received his MFA from the Vermont College of Fine Arts. His work has appeared in *About Place, Barrelhouse, Bellevue Literary Review, Briar Cliff Review, Cutthroat, Feral,* and *ZYZZYVA.* He lives in New Mexico.

Essay

NFL Road Trip

Michael Graham

I prefer to travel by book. Paul Theroux has taken me from Cairo to Capetown in Africa. With Jonathan Raban aboard his 35-foot sailboat, we navigated the 1,000-mile Inside Passage from Seattle to Juneau. There was a memorable journey years ago with Bruce Chatwin to "the far end of the world," as the restless Brit described Patagonia, the vast, rugged territory at the tip of South America. Travel by book is the way to go, especially these days. It's cheaper, whether going by hardcover or paperback. You don't need to mask-up. You avoid the TSA lines that snake through airports, the ubiquitous orange barrels on the interstate highways. You kick back in your recliner while the author deals with the linguistic barriers and sweats out the nasty microbial infections in foreign countries. Annoying tourists always seem to find Theroux. Chatwin, in Patagonia, hitched a ride with a Chilean truck driver whose feet, he reported, "smelled like cheese."

So, in January when my wife Linda said our daughter in Georgia had called, inviting us to join her and her fiancé in Nashville for the upcoming NFL divisional playoff game between the Tennessee Titans and our hometown Cincinnati Bengals, I was not properly enthusiastic. Instead, I began finding reasons why we shouldn't make what would be a quick weekend trip, the game just four hours and fifteen minutes down the road. Yes, but you know people drive too fast on the freeway. It's the middle of winter, we'll freeze our septuagenarian asses off. Our seats are field-level, we'll have to stand the entire time. You know pro football fans — the Dawg Pound in Cleveland, the Jungle in Cincinnati, it doesn't matter where — they're intolerable. Yada, yada, yada.

The more excuses I made, the less convincing I sounded. Even I didn't buy my argument for staying home, not after the Bengals had just defeated the Las Vegas Raiders in the opening round of the playoffs, touching off a weeklong end zone celebration, if you will, in Cincinnati. "Act like you've been there before," the late Paul Brown was known to say when one of his players would do a touchdown dance or spike the ball after scoring. Yet it had been thirty-one years since the club that Brown founded had won a playoff game. Bengals fans were understandably charged up, my spouse included. Linda would be going to Nashville, with or without her complaining, worry-wart husband. She hadn't been this excited since the last time we attended a Bengals playoff game together — way, way back at Super Bowl XVI in Pontiac, Michigan, where Forrest Gregg's squad lost to quarterback Joe Montana and the San Francisco 49ers. It was bitterly cold in Pontiac too, but the 1982 game was played inside, under a dome, and as the Bengals beat reporter for *The Cincinnati Post* I had a comfortable seat in the pressbox, far from the madding crowd. *The Post* folded in 2007, a casualty of declining readership in afternoon papers around the country. I folded too, leaving the business in 1989. There would be no press pass this time.

We arrived in the Music City on Friday, the day before the game, a cold front blowing into town ahead of us. The forecast for Saturday called for highs only in the mid-30s, sunny skies, and a 100 percent chance of Derrick Henry. "The King," as his loyal subjects in Tennessee bow to their All-Pro running back, would be returning to the field after being sidelined for two months with a foot injury. Bad news for the Bengals. For us, the news was all good. Our weekend stay at The Joseph, a Marriott boutique hotel within walking distance of Nashville's honky tonks and the Titans' stadium, would be fully comped by our daughter's fiancé — much appreciated after the valet who parked my car said the rate was $56 a day. When one of the beaming clerks who checked us in at the front desk offered Linda and me each a mini teacup of chai latte, I decided maybe it was finally time to lose my shamefully bad attitude and warm up a little to this experience I'd be sharing with family and Bengals fans. (Just don't ask me to wear stripes. Silly as it seems, I try to maintain at least the appearance of objectivity, even if it was half a lifetime ago when I covered the club. I still can't look at the expensive Waterford crystal bowl Linda and I received as a wedding gift from Paul Brown and not feel compromised in some way.)

The staff at The Joseph treated us like visiting dignitaries, so willing to be of service that when I decided I needed a softer bed pillow, I told Linda that management would probably dispatch a valet to Cincinnati to pluck mine off the bed in our townhouse and drive it back to Nashville if I asked them to do so. As it was, they sent up three different pillows for me to try. What our friendly, eager-to-please hosts couldn't provide, unfortunately, was a hard copy of a newspaper — not even a print edition of the local *Tennessean*. When I asked the concierge where I could find the *New York Times* (other than on my Android), she shrugged and pointed across the street. "Try Dunkin' Donuts."

I woke up Saturday morning and decided to grab a cup of coffee at the Starbucks in the hotel around the corner. Maybe I could get my hands on a newspaper there. It was 6 a.m. when I left our room on the 16th floor and walked down the dark hallway to the bank of elevators, not a soul stirring. Cincinnati fans and Tennessee fans wouldn't be putting on their game faces until later that afternoon, trudging elbow-to-elbow across the John Seigenthaler Pedestrian Bridge over the Cumberland River for the three o'clock kickoff in

Nissan Stadium. The half-mile-long bridge is named after the late editor of the *Tennessean*, who, as a young reporter with the paper, saved a suicidal man from jumping off the bridge — a leap the disconsolate might have considered taking after their top-seeded Titans were upset, 19-16, by the Bengals.

Waiting that morning on an elevator descending from the 20th floor, I stared at the video art on the far wall. A tree toppled over in a forest, begging the question that philosophers have debated for centuries. The video, however, ran silently in a slow-motion loop, this tree not making a sound while I stood there watching it fall through the woods, nor would it have made a sound had I been back in my room and out of earshot. In retrospect, I now see the video as a portent, the falling tree a foreshadowing of the calamitous events on the field that day, events the Bengals somehow managed to overcome. Joe Burrow, their second-year quarterback, went down again and again under the Titans' fierce pass rush — sacked nine times, a playoff record the Bengals' permeable offensive line shared with the Titans' defensive front. Burrow's so-called pass protectors could only help their unflappable QB to his feet after each hit and hope he would keep making plays when the team desperately needed plays to be made. The game ended with a Burrow pass that set up placekicker Evan McPherson, who booted a 52-yard field goal as time expired. The rookie called his winning kick before launching it — a la Babe Ruth pointing to the centerfield wall at Wrigley Field before famously hitting a home run in the 1932 World Series — and thereafter his moniker was "Money" McPherson as the Bengals made their unlikely pilgrimage to the Super Bowl.

What I couldn't stop talking about, though, after returning home from this trip I didn't want to make, was another startling moment, a spooky encounter that Rod Serling could have introduced in one of his monologues from his 1960s TV series "The Twilight Zone." *There is a fifth dimension beyond that which is known to man... a dimension as vast as space and timeless as infinity... the dimension of the imagination... an area we call the Twilight Zone.* That's where I seemed to be when the elevator door opened early that morning and standing in the corner, all alone, was Mike Vrabel, the head coach of the Tennessee Titans. All 6-4 of him. No mask. Stubby beard. He could have been a ghost, a swirling hologram. The valet, the front desk clerk, the concierge who sent me across the street to the donut shop, had not said a word — there was not a peep, in fact, out of anybody — about the Titans being quarantined in our hotel, if indeed Vrabel and his players really had spent the night there, segregated from the public as mandated by the NFL while the SARS-CoV-2 virus remained on the loose. Yet there he was, the Ohio State All-American, the New England Patriots linebacker, the NFL Coach of the Year in 2021, looking directly at me. I've seen that look of apprehension before, when VIPs are afraid you might accost them and ask for an autograph, or worse, try to make conversation.

"Good luck today," I said, getting on the elevator.

Vrabel nodded.

The door closed. We began going down.

Elevator rides with strangers are always uncomfortable. This one was uncomfortable and weird.

"I'm from Cincinnati. I used to cover the Bengals in the Munoz and Collinsworth days," I said, a remark that surely made no sense because I had failed to identify myself as a has-been reporter.

Vrabel nodded again. We stopped at the 8th floor. *What can I say before he gets off?*

"I'm a big Ohio State fan." *Weak, Michael. Weak.*

The door opened. With one last nod, Vrabel was gone.

When I returned to the room with my coffee, I told Linda I had ridden on the elevator with the Titans' coach, just the two of us, and was so stunned to be face-to-face with him I sounded like a silly, awestruck fan. We joked about the one-sided conversation. I should have hit the emergency stop button, demanded Vrabel hand over the Titans' gameplan. I should have told him I saw his running back in the hotel bar late last night and he appeared to be limping. (The King carried the ball 20 times, gained 62 yards, and scored one TD — yeoman's work, but not spectacular.) I should have asked the question I'd been asking since I arrived. "I'm looking for a newspaper, Coach. Do you know where I can find one?"

Michael Graham is director of operations for Zeigler Financial, a financial services firm in Wilmington, Ohio. He resides in Cincinnati, where he was a staff writer for *Cincinnati Magazine* (1989-96) and a reporter for *The Cincinnati Post* (1976-85). His sportswriting portfolio includes five seasons as the *Post*'s reporter on the Cincinnati Bengals beat and a year as the paper's sports columnist, traveling around the country to cover a wide range of events, including the 1984 Summer Olympics in Los Angeles. At *Cincinnati Magazine*, he specialized in profiles of the Queen City's major sports figures, politicians, media personalities, entertainers, and business leaders.

Poetry

After the Catch
John Monagle

What you saw on the video
when I was pounded to the turf
by the linebacker two steps
after I caught the pass from
the quarterback is not how it was.

After I caught Kyle's pass,
Bill "The Bull" Grigson
collided with my mid-section.

I floated three feet above the grass
for half an hour. Other players
came towards me in slow motion.
I held the football
as if it were a baby or a bomb.

I laid on the field, wanting
to let go of the ball and my arm
to fall lifelessly onto the surface.
I wanted at least two years to breathe
my next breath but couldn't let myself
be covered under a shroud of moans.

It was not what you see on the recording,
where once I was tackled,
I quickly got up and handed the ball
to the official, then returned to the huddle.

Mitchell came in for me with the play
the team was to run next. I jogged
to the sidelines, and sat on the bench.

My insides were like trees flattened
by a meteor, branches and leaves limp
on the ground, trunk embedded in earth.

John Monagle resides in Las Cruces, New Mexico. He's retired from working at The Library of Congress. He is a graduate of Vermont College of Fine Arts with a MFA in creative writing, specializing in poetry. He has had numerous poems published in a variety of journals and anthologies, most recently in the forthcoming *2022 New Mexico Poet Laureate Anthology*, *Coffin Bell*, and *Agape Review*, as well as a previously published poem in *Sport Literate*.

Poetry

Football Tailgate as Anthropolgy: Field Notes

Remi Recchia

Observation #49: We are the only conspicuously gay tent.

Observation #21: The tuba player is fat. The color guard is thin. Look closer to see how they are all the same.

Observation #56: A tall man wears school spirit overalls. I suspect he is not a farmer and thus has no need for overalls. Then again, I am also not a farmer.

Observation #4: I see Matthew Shepard when I look in the mirror. I am not Matthew Shepard but at a different time and in a different place I could be.

Observation #12: I have never seen so much booze in one place before, and I was raised in a brewery. I rub my 90-day chip between my thumb and forefinger like a rosary.

Observation #40: It may rain soon. I hear the ambulance across town.

Observation #33: At the middle school youth quake, I was informed to let the Lord wash over me. All I wanted to stand in was the tidal wave of another man.

Observation #62: My friend Mark is frail but exuberant, and, I'm guessing, wearing a rainbow thong. My friend Paul woke up blacked-out. My friend Peter brought the deck of cards. They're an heirloom from his parents.

Yes, I am naming Apostles now.

Observation #15: Thunder merges with a grackle's mating call.

Observation #39: The policemen on horses do not deter the crowd. It is almost as if the policemen on horses are not welcome. ACAB, we shout in glee. ACAB. ACAB.

Observation #47: My friend Paul is so drunk I could steal his nose right off his face. I don't steal his nose, but I am reminded of our first kiss at the house party. The lights were loud and I could taste the music in my mouth. My molars hurt. His face has always been elegant.

Observation #90: I never prayed to be different but I prayed to forget. The forgetting begat a DUI. The DUI begat a court date. The court date begat second helpings of shame.

Observation #65: It is five hours until kickoff. I want to tell a joke about the last time I got off, but I can't remember the punchline.

American Airlines always pats me down extra.

Observation #17: The air can't decide if it's wet or ice-dry. It kisses up my calves like a snake, like a man. It knows what's waiting there. I won't charge it just to look.

Observation #3: The sky yellows. The crowd bellows. The game, like many things, is cancelled.

Observation #80: The policemen's horses let out useless shits on the pavement. The police, generally speaking, are useless.

When did ghosts decide to keep silent?

Observation #72: I would rather be huddled in this shelter, counting the premature whiskers on Mark's face, than throwing up in a dive bar, but here I am doing both. Except this time it's not my vomit, it's everyone else's, and the shelter is the dive bar and heaven is hell and Rilke was right: every angel is terrifying.

But wait: my body is an angel and my friends' bodies are angels and every body that has ever come before our bodies is an angel, spreading feathered wings against AIDS and Prop 8 and Wyoming fence posts, swallowing broken teeth in the face of an elephant grave and wishing, always, for the game to stop.

Remi Recchia is a trans poet and essayist from Kalamazoo, Michigan. He is a PhD candidate in English-Creative Writing at Oklahoma State University. He currently serves as an associate editor for the *Cimarron Review*. A four-time Pushcart Prize nominee, Remi's work has appeared or will soon appear in *Best New Poets 2021*, *Columbia Online Journal*, *Harpur Palate*, and *Juked*, among others. He holds an MFA in poetry from Bowling Green State University. Remi is the author of *Quicksand/Stargazing* (Cooper Dillon Books, 2021).

Book Excerpt

Blackballed: Race, the NBA, and the Eastern Professional Basketball League

Syl Sobel and Jay Rosenstein

The following is partially excerpted from Boxed Out of the NBA: Remembering the Eastern Professional Basketball League.

Most sports fans — and even non-fans — know the history of integration in professional baseball. Jackie Robinson broke the color barrier in Major League Baseball in 1947. Before that, African Americans who wanted to play professional baseball were restricted to the Negro Leagues. But what about the color line in professional basketball? Who was the first African American pioneer? What, if any, avenues were open to African Americans who wanted to play pro basketball before Blacks were allowed into the NBA and even after, when their numbers remained small? Was there a basketball equivalent to the Negro Leagues?

During the early years of organized basketball in the first half of the 20th century, professional basketball was segregated like most of life in the United States. As author Mark Johnson described in his book, *Basketball Slave*, the early days of pro basketball were characterized by independent barnstorming teams rather than by organized leagues. These independent teams played against each other, against local amateur teams, and all other comers — but the teams were either all-Black or all-white, not integrated. All-white teams would sometimes compete against all-Black teams, but there were no professional leagues in which Black and white professional players competed either with or against each other.

The first two major professional basketball leagues were the American Basketball League (ABL), which began in 1925, and the National Basketball League (NBL), which started in 1937. They, too, were all-white. But even as these leagues were getting established, segregated independent teams continued to compete and remained popular — in many cases more popular than their counterparts in the NBL and ABL.

The most accomplished of the all-black independent teams of that era was the New York Renaissance Big Five, who were also known as the New York Rens and the Harlem Rens. In 1939, the Rens won the inaugural

World Professional Basketball Championship sponsored by the *Chicago Herald American* newspaper, beating the NBL's Oshkosh All-Stars, 34-25. John Wooden, the legendary UCLA coach who played during the 1930s with the barnstorming Indianapolis Kautskys, reportedly said of the Rens, "I have never seen a team play better team basketball."

The following year another all-Black independent club, the Harlem Globetrotters — in the days before they became known primarily for their showmanship — won the championship, and in 1943 another all-Black independent team, the Washington Bears, composed mostly of players from the Rens, also won. Otherwise, all-white NBL teams won the rest of the tournaments, which ended in 1949 when the NBL and the Basketball Association of America (BAA), which was launched in 1946, merged to form the NBA.

The Rens and Globetrotters were the most popular — and arguably the best — teams in professional basketball. They drew large crowds wherever they played and offered a faster-paced, more exciting, and fan-pleasing brand of basketball than the white professional leagues.

The first of the major professional leagues to integrate was the NBL. In 1942, with many pro basketball players off to World War II, the Toledo and Chicago franchises signed several African American players to fill out their rosters, including several Globetrotters. Bill Jones of Toledo is generally considered the first African American to play on an integrated team.

Four more Black players joined the NBL in 1946, including William "Pop" Gates, the star of those world champion Rens and Bears teams. Gates, however, got into a fight with a Syracuse player during a game which, according to newspaper reports, nearly triggered a riot, and the Blackhawks dropped Gates before the end of the season. Other NBL teams did the same with their Black players — ironically, just a few months before the April 1947 debut of Jackie Robinson in Major League Baseball.

The NBL tried another form of integration in 1948-49, inviting the Rens to replace the financially troubled Detroit Vagabond Kings, who had folded early in the season. The Rens accepted, moved the franchise to Ohio, and became the Dayton Rens. They finished out the season in the NBL as the first all-Black team in organized professional basketball, with Gates as player/coach.

The ABL also took its first baby steps toward integration in 1948. John "Boy Wonder" Isaacs, another star of those world champion Rens and Bears squads, played part of the 1948-49 season with Brooklyn. Then, after the NBL's Dayton Rens experiment ended in 1949, Gates joined the ABL's Scranton Miners, as did former Ren and Washington Bear William "Dolly" King and several other African American players.

"It wasn't that easy at first, my grandfather said, to have that many Blacks," said Brian Maloney, grandson of Miners' owner Joseph "Speed" Maloney. "I know my grandfather got some heat from people for bringing in [Black players]. . . . That was talked about, and it was talked about in the fashion that you're keeping a white boy from getting a [job]." However, Maloney said, the fans quickly came around, especially "once they started putting the ball in the hoop, if they were winning."

Win they did. The Miners would win the ABL title in 1949-50 and 1950-51.

The NBA finally broke its color barrier in 1950, allowing three Black players into the league: Chuck Cooper (Boston Celtics), Nat "Sweetwater" Clifton (New York Knicks), and Earl Lloyd (Washington Capitals). A fourth, Hank Dezonie (Tri-Cities Blackhawks), joined the league after the season started. Cooper, Clifton, and Dezonie were former Globetrotters, and Lloyd had been working out with the 'Trotters before he was drafted to the NBA.

Integration would come slowly to the NBA during the 1950s and early 1960s, however. According to figures compiled by Johnson, the league would not have more than nine black players in any one season until 1956-57, when it had 14 among its eight teams.

Meanwhile, six weeks before the BAA formed in 1946, the Eastern Professional Basketball League was organized in Hazleton, Pennsylvania, by a group of Eastern Pennsylvania semi-pro basketball team owners who wanted to upgrade the quality of play and professionalism. The league would play weekend games only and had ambitions of serving as a minor league to the major professional leagues.

In that first season, the Eastern League had three Black players, all on the Hazleton Mountaineers: Zach Clayton, John Isaacs, and William "Rookie" Brown — all veterans of the Black barnstorming teams. Isaacs played only that one season in the EBL, but Clayton and Brown remained in the league for at least the next year, with Brown being selected second-team all-league. Also in 1947-48, former Globetrotter and Ren Frank Washington played for the league's Philadelphia Lumberjacks.

In the early 1950s, several players implicated in the 1951 college basketball point-shaving scandal and banned from the NBA for life, including Sherman White, Ed Warner, Floyd Lane, and Bob McDonald, along with former Philadelphia high school star Bob Gainey joined the league. With that, doors opened for Black players much more quickly in the EBL than in the NBA.

Black players not only faced limited opportunities to get into the NBA, the few who made it there also were expected to play limited roles.

In 1955-56, the Hazleton Hawks became the first integrated professional basketball league team with an all-Black starting lineup: White, Layne, Tom Hemans, Jesse Arnelle, and Fletcher Johnson. The NBA would not have an all-Black starting lineup for another nine years — the 1964 Celtics — and after that, not until the 1971 Milwaukee Bucks.

By 1960, with the NBA about 20 percent Black, the Eastern League was seen as predominantly black. As reported by Ron Thomas in *They Cleared the Lane: The NBA's Black Pioneers*, one of the Allentown Jets' owners, John Kimock, estimated the league was about 70 percent black in the early 1960s.

As Mark Johnson — whose father, Andy, was a former Globetrotter who played three years in the NBA — wrote: "In the 1950s and '60s, the NBA was letting Black players in — in Noah-like fashion, two by two." Or, as many former Eastern League players and observers put it, the NBA had an unwritten but implicit quota on the number of Black players per team of no more than two players, which gradually increased over time.

"When I got out of Niagara in 1956, it was widely known and practiced that NBA teams limited the number of Black players on each NBA team," said Hemans, a member of that all-Black starting five in Hazleton and a 15-year Eastern League veteran. "Without question race was the major factor that kept talented Black basketball players out of the NBA."

"They already knew who was going to play and who wasn't going to play," recalled Cleveland "Swish" McKinney of the St. Louis Hawks' training camp during the preseason of 1964. McKinney had been an all-Army player and was on the Pan American Games winning team of 1963 with future NBA star Willis Reed among others. "You could come on a team, and you look around [at the number of Black players]," and wonder, "Aww, jeez, am I going to make this here?"

"Quotas existed," said sportswriter and commentator Bob Ryan, who grew up an Eastern League fan in Trenton, New Jersey. "Nobody can deny it."

Black players not only faced limited opportunities to get into the NBA, the few who made it there also were expected to play limited roles.

Earl Lloyd, who in 1950 became the first African-American to play in an NBA game, recalled in his autobiography, *Moonfixer: The Basketball Journey of Earl Lloyd*, that "nobody said it, but it was whispered how most of the Black guys who made it early in the NBA were big, physical guys who weren't expected to be cerebral. They let white guys run the team on the floor, and they sent the Black guys under the hoop to do the heavy labor, which fit the pattern in this country for a long, long time."

The NBA's rejection of talented Black players was the Eastern League's gain. It "created a pool of highly talented Black players, many of whom had starred at various highly ranked colleges," said Hemans, a Niagara graduate who had an offer to play for Cincinnati in the NBA but declined when they refused to guarantee his contract.

From the mid-1950s until the formation of the American Basketball Association in 1967, the Eastern League had many of the top African American players in the country, especially scorers. The top four scorers in Eastern League history, and eight of the top 10, were African Americans.

The league's stars included Black players from top college programs such as Hemans, Julius McCoy (Michigan State), Hal "King" Lear (Temple), Wally Choice (Indiana), Dick Gaines (Seton Hall), Sherman White (Long Island University), and Hank Whitney (Iowa State). Other stars came from HBCU's, such as Roman Turmon (Clark), Chaney (Bethune-Cookman), Walt Simon (Benedict), and Waite Bellamy (Florida A&M). Stacey Arceneaux, a New York City high school legend recruited to Iowa State, never played there but became the second-highest scorer in Eastern League history. Ray Scott left Portland after one year and played three seasons in the Eastern League before becoming an NBA and ABA star and later coach of the Detroit Pistons.

"All of these players were great in their own right," said John Chaney, former Temple coach. "They should have been [in the NBA]. It's a darn shame. . . . I would have to say that people like that [were] kept from reaching their level that they should have."

"It was a different world in those days," said Ryan.

"You don't have to be incredibly brilliant to figure out what was going on," said Scott, who lived and played through it.

Many Black former Eastern League players from the late 1950s and early 1960s who are mentioned as NBA-caliber talents were dynamic individual players who stood out — and that was the problem.

Consider the case of Cleo Hill. Hill, a multi-talented 6-1 guard from tiny Winston-Salem State University in North Carolina, could run the floor, score from outside and inside, leap, rebound, and block shots — and do it all with flair. As Thomas wrote, "[o]f the many black players who should have been but weren't in the NBA, Cleo Hill is spoken of in almost Jordan-esque terms."

> "Quotas existed," said sportswriter and basketball commentator Bob Ryan, who grew up an Eastern League fan in Trenton. "Nobody can deny it."

The St. Louis Hawks drafted Hill eighth in the first round of the 1961 NBA draft and brought him to training camp. What happened from there has been the subject of various articles and a segment in the ESPN documentary Black Magic about African-Americans and basketball.

Hill dazzled in training camp with his multiple talents, including his outside shot, which the Hawks sorely needed. Unfortunately for Hill, he joined a veteran team anchored by its "Big Three" star frontcourt players, Bob Pettit, Cliff Hagan, and Clyde Lovellete. As various versions of the story go, at some point during the preseason the team's veterans became unhappy because Hill's speediness and scoring ability cut into their scoring opportunities, and because of the attention Hill was getting for his exciting style of play.

The veterans reportedly complained to Hawks' owner Ben Kerner, who sided with them and told Seymour to cut Hill's playing time. Seymour refused and, 14 games into the season, Kerner fired him. Hill, after starting the season averaging almost 11 PPG under Seymour, finished the season as a part-time player and, his confidence shot, averaged 5.5 PPG. The following year the Hawks cut Hill in training camp. He ended up playing five seasons in the Eastern League and would never play in the NBA again.

To African-American players of that era, the Cleo Hill story was a cautionary tale, a reminder of what could happen at that time to a black athlete who dared to shine. Said Ray Scott:

> That was my first year in the NBA. So not only did I hear about it, I saw it — part of it — because Cleo and I were first-round picks, and so I knew how good he was and his capability. This was the days when you wanted basketball players, you did not want athletes. And Cleo was a

hybrid. . . . Speed, strength, quickness. So when combining all those elements, putting it with guys who wanted to play a step slower — they didn't want to play at the pace that Cleo excelled at — then obviously we know the rest. And it's a tragedy. I mean to me it's a Shakespearean tragedy because it really affects someone's life.

In contrast to the NBA, race generally did not seem to be a significant factor in determining who made it into the Eastern League, at least not by the 1960s. Allentown owner Kimock told Thomas: "There was no discrimination as far as [Eastern League] club owners were concerned. . . . Everybody wanted to win a championship. I think if you went with a solid white team, it would have finished last."

Scranton owner "Art Pachter wanted the best ballplayers on the floor at any time, and he had great coaches that wanted the best ballplayers," said Willie Somerset, a Duquesne grad who starred in the Eastern League and ABA. "He wanted the best team, and the best team filled up the coliseums and the arenas."

"I don't ever remember anybody having any thoughts about race in the Eastern League, to be honest with you," said George Blaney, who played in the league in the 1960s before launching a distinguished college coaching career. "You know, Black players started, Black players played hard, but I can't remember any quotas or anything."

This isn't to say the league was entirely color-blind in assembling its teams.

"We had many, many good white players," Bellamy said. "Many excellent white players. We did have the same kind of situation, though. We always wanted to keep a few white players on each team whether they sat on the bench or what."

And by all accounts, race was not an issue for the players either on or off the court. Players carpooled together, shared motel rooms on the road, and often formed friendships off the court.

Recalled Somerset: "We didn't think about discrimination or who was on the ballclub or who was not. We were just concerned about winning."

By the mid-1960s, the NBA was integrated and the quotas had ended. NBA fans had become accustomed to watching and rooting for Black players. Teams seeing the success of the Celtics sought to compete. In 1967, when the ABA emerged and needed good players to fill their rosters, teams looked for the best ballplayers they could find — including some 30 Eastern Leaguers, most of them Black. Such players were perfectly suited for the

ABA's up-tempo, entertaining style, and had played with a three-point line in the Eastern League since 1964.

"The ABA was an outgrowth of the '60s social revolution," Scott observed. "The NBA began in the era of accepted '40s segregation. The NBA moved the needle in 1950. The ABA was the needle."

Looking back, Scott said, "That whole basketball world has changed. . . . You know, it was unthinkable that on a team of 10 players, that eight of them would be African Americans."

Said Chaney:

There were so many great players that certainly were capable of playing in the NBA . . . I thought there were great players that should have been in the NBA, but they neglected to recruit them. ... Racist views held this country in a position where it couldn't move. This country could have moved a lot faster... the world, a lot faster if it was able to get rid of these issues. . . . There was so much talent that was lost because of these social issues that tend to get in the way of people being successful. It's a shame. It's a shame.

Syl Sobel is an author, attorney, and journalist. In addition to *Boxed Out of the NBA: Remembering the Eastern Professional Basketball League*, he has written a series of children's books on U.S. history and civics, including books on the Constitution, the Declaration of Independence, and presidential elections. He is an op ed contributor to newspapers and has covered high school sports for a community newspaper. Sobel spent 31 years as director of publications for a federal government agency.

Jay Rosenstein is a writer/editor who in 1977 began his career as a reporter for the daily financial newspaper *American Banker*. He primarily covered Congress, federal agencies, and consumer and financial issues. Rosenstein continued his career as a senior writer/editor for a federal government agency for more than 30 years. He is currently retired and is working on a children's book.

Poetry

Three at Home, Four on the Road, Five When You're Behind

Flavian Mark Lupinetti

Every so often we ran the play like Father Pete taught us, with our
center Muhammad snagging the rebound and hitting one of us
scrappy Italian kids on the wing, dribbling only once before passing
to Malcolm Brown, "The Best in Town" according to Malcolm Brown,
and Malcolm hitting Jimmy Jeter at the foul line, Jimmy whose brother
played for the Pistons, making Jimmy royalty among us 12-year-olds,
and Jimmy feeding Peachy Miller, holding the ball for barely a second,
waiting for the defender to commit, then dishing back to Jimmy
racing the rock to the rack for an easy layup. When the opposing coach
called time, Father Pete glowed like he saw the Beatific Vision.
You ran that fast break perfect, boys. Just like St. Paul drew it up.

Our little town's neighborhoods were segregated. Our elementary schools too.
Our only public swimming pool never dampened a black body.
But our church league basketball team epitomized racial harmony.

We opened the '65 season thumping the Lutherans by 22, the Methodists by 17.
Father Pete made us take it easy on the Blessed Virgin. We beat her by only 9.
Father Pete gave me more playing time than I deserved.
He declared me *gritty*. He praised my *unselfish play*.
He admired my *deceptive speed*. He called me his *coach on the court*.

I didn't fully understand his coaching philosophy until our second game against the Presbyterians, when because of colds and sprains only seven of us suited up. Playing in the Presbyterians' gym, surrounded by their friends and family, the heathens battled back after trailing by ten at the half. With two minutes left in the third quarter and the game tied, Father Pete told me to hold the ball for the last shot. With ten seconds left I tried to hit Peachy as he cut to the hole, but the damn infidel guarding him intercepted and broke for the basket. I had no choice but to foul, my fifth of the game.

That meant that to start the fourth quarter, Father Pete had to choose between Eddie DiBacco, who couldn't shoot for shit, and what he lacked in offensive prowess, he compensated for with indifferent defense, or Ronnie Jefferson, whose cousin Timmy played cornerback at Ohio State, and in two years would shut down OJ Simpson in OJ's first Rose Bowl.

Eddie D, said Father Pete. Go get 'em, tiger. Win it for the one true church. When Father Pete caught me staring, he winked. He drew me close. He whispered. *You always need one white guy out there. To calm 'em down.*

Flavian Mark Lupinetti, a poet, fiction writer, cardiac surgeon, and former wrestling coach, received his MFA from the Vermont College of Fine Arts. His work has appeared in *About Place, Barrelhouse, Bellevue Literary Review, Briar Cliff Review, Cutthroat, Feral,* and *ZYZZYVA*. He lives in New Mexico.

Poetry

We Know the Truth About Bones

Pam Sinicrope

Court fourteen at the Rochester Athletic Club —
five goslings peep and a mother
goose hisses from the other side of the fence.

And just beyond that, beyond a small bog,
on a high school parking lot, a tiny band marches
out-of-sync with snare drums. Merciless

on clay, my son spirals
balls over the net while I choose
to return on the rise or retreat. Should I

let him win? Every time I forget
to split-step, my knees scream until I
remember to forget I have

a body. Inside this grey box I feel
nothing but the pleasure
of follow through and return —

the reason I still play. He tries to beat me
with better strokes, but I'm gristle and instinct — a mother
goose who fights, beak-bared and bent

through wind and sun. Thwack after thwack,
we know what to do here. Only here.
God this boy — so splendid — his spins

like Rafa at Rolland Garros —
fly out and back. I can't connect.
I feel like a sixth-grader herr-onking

a french horn, bones bruising bones.
We know the truth about mothers with bad knees.
He's beginning to know himself.

That's When You Know

What does it take to win? First
serve. Stand just behind the baseline
but never in the same spot. Always
bounce the ball five times.

Let an opponent see your eyes, know you
know their quirks. Stare too long and lose
rhythm. And when you toss, let the ball
fly as if releasing a dove.

But if it smacks the net, untuck
another one from your skirt
for a fresh start that doesn't hold
the memory of your miss. Aim

for angle on a slow twirl, advance
toward the service line, then volley.
Some say tennis is mental,
but might as well call it ritual,

the way minds spin
to swing, split-step, lunge. Forget
the score, might as well call it a revelation,
how you forget frayed cartilage, your forearm

stuck with dry needles, and the crutches
you hobbled on for months.
Forget yourself, might as well call it
compulsion, the way you ache

to return. Here, you are simply sun
— bliss and blood. You give
arc and twirl. As long as you can —
you get twirl and arc.

Pam Sinicrope lives in Rochester, Minnesota. She has an MFA from Augsburg University and is a senior poetry editor for *RockPaperPoem*. Her poems appeared in *Aethlon, SWWIM, Spillway,* and *3 Elements Review*. She enjoys family time, hiking with her dog, and tennis.

Poetry

1932

Kate Wylie

Babe Ruth's smart feet
squared up to the plate, he pointed
then homered
to clinch game three for the Yankees. I had just been born
upstate. Every birthday when I was young, my father recounted
Babe Ruth's big-bodied but humble swagger, his induction
into the Hall of Fame. *Inaugural class of inductees* my father said
year after year, turn-of-the-century eyes shining. And I,
as skeptical first daughters do, pressed: *how
did Babe do it, though?*

My mother jumped in there to deem it
an act of faith. My father almost always deferred to her
but sometimes defended it as good reflexes
or wind. He was practical,
came to America and started a potato farm
in New York, a sure bet. He only drank
on holidays. We split turkey wishbones
and rooted for the Yankees and prayed to God
the night Babe Ruth died. I was sixteen and still
wondered if the point was miracle or malarkey. One night
many years later, my father died too, in his comfortable armchair
right after dinner, the daily racing form folded
over his knee like he was just starting or ending
and it could have been either.

Kate Wylie (she/they) is a poetry MFA candidate at Pacific University and 2018 Webster University alum. Wylie reads fiction for *The New Southern Fugitives,* regularly contributes to the Ehlers-Danlos Syndrome society magazine *Loose Connections,* and has published work in literary magazines including *Canary, October Hill Magazine, Visitant,* and *Sport Literate.*

YOUR LEISURELY CARRIAGE AWAITS

Sport Literate back issues available online: www.sportliterate.org. Or, better yet, subscribe (two issues for just $20) and get what's new.

Essay

The List
Todd Morgan

Sam and I were having lunch at the kitchen table. His baseball cap shielded his eyes as he leaned over a piece of paper, pencil grasped in his small hand, his PB&J partly eaten.

"What's that?" I said.

He didn't look up.

"Coach said if he was going to war, he'd take some of the guys with him, but some of us he wouldn't."

I put down my newspaper and peered across the table. I saw a partial listing of his teammates' names: Matt, Ricky, …. My 9-year-old was trying to figure out which group he fell in. Go to war or be left at home?

I felt a sudden urge to shield him.

The young coach who said this, Nick, had a swagger about him, one that was either contagious or obnoxious depending on whether you were associated with his team or the opposition. A star high school athlete just a few years earlier, he wore mirrored sunglasses and shaved his head. The kids idolized him.

Like most coaches, Nick had a deep competitive streak. But unlike most coaches, he seemed to know how to fully embrace competition while keeping things in perspective. Time after time he steeled the team to rally from a deficit. He would build up the confidence of each batter, one pitch at a time. For a boy intent on driving in a run, he'd call out, "Just make contact." To boost a kid battling deep in the count, he'd yell, "Good at bat." If a pitcher challenged a baserunner's lead, well then, on the next pitch Nick would shout to the boy to take an even bigger lead. It was a master class in pitting one's will against the opponent.

Then, once the game ended and he had talked to the team about lessons learned, his intensity vanished. Lighthearted and matter-of-fact behind the mirrored shades, he would crank up the volume on his car stereo and head off into the afternoon blasting "We Like to Party! (The Vengabus)."

There's a photo I love of Greg taken in Saigon in 1968. It's a head shot of him in jungle fatigues. He's wearing a boonie hat and standard issue glasses. The freckles across the bridge of his nose remind me of Sam.

Why was this good coach challenging these young boys with a misguided war analogy? Might one of them quietly conclude at 9 or 10 years old that he was a coward? Was I overreacting?

Sam loved sports, and I wanted to help him be successful. We enjoyed tossing the ball back and forth. I bought him an expensive aluminum bat. Sometimes I pitched to him, or we went to the batting cages and then got hot dogs afterward. Occasionally I cleaned caked mud off his cleats at night after he was asleep and wondered if I was too invested. But there were plenty of other parents like my wife and me, who went to every game and followed each pitch.

When I was Sam's age, my brother Greg enlisted in an intelligence branch of the Army. The enlistment officer told him that because he'd be schooled in top secret codes, he'd never be sent to a combat zone, so he'd never be in jeopardy of revealing secrets if captured and tortured. Greg was pleased and thought he had sidestepped Vietnam. The officer's story, while plausible and correct in the small details, was a stunning lie.

I often studied the photo that sat on top of the TV while Greg was gone: my parents and him standing next to each other at the airport, my mom with red eyes, my dad wearing a suit and a grim expression, my brother frowning in his dress uniform with its few ribbon medals. Before the Army, Greg wore oxford-cloth shirts, drank Pepsi, smoked a pipe, read *Playboy*, and listened to Dave Brubeck.

When he came home, he drank beer, smoked pot, worked 'fuck' and its variations into almost every conversation, and listened to The Band, Dylan, and Jimi Hendrix. He told me a story about a highly decorated soldier who did something violent and obscene to a cat. He taught me I could solve life's problems just by saying "fuck it." From all of this I understood war was a kind of betrayal or, as Greg would have put it, a complete fucking mess.

There's a photo I love of Greg taken in Saigon in 1968. It's a head shot of him in jungle fatigues. He's wearing a boonie hat and standard issue glasses. The freckles across the bridge of his nose remind me of Sam. His blue eyes stare with childlike determination as he sticks out his tongue at the camera.

I had never considered Sam going to war until Nick's comment triggered me like an unexpected muscle memory. I doubt I could've tempered my response to Sam if I'd known that ultimately Greg would die of ALS. It's a brutal disease that progressively weakens the muscles, including ones you didn't know you had. Near the end, Greg couldn't even close his eyes. The causes of ALS are unknown, but veterans are twice as likely to get it as the general population. The U.S. government presumes there's a service connection when a vet gets the disease.

To try to convey my attitude to a nine-year-old focused on baseball would have been foolish. At the same time, it was insidiously easy to challenge a kid to jump on the war bandwagon and thereby plant seeds of moral confusion about what war is — and isn't. I also feared one day Sam might have a life-changing conversation with an army recruiter, possibly a charismatic young man with a shaved head and sunglasses.

"Sam... Nick doesn't know you well enough to say something like that."

The baseball cap tipped up and Sam looked out for a moment. It seemed he registered what I said though there was a distant look in his eyes. Then, he returned to pondering the list.

Watching Sam hunkered down, I faced the fact that I would be on guard but he would make his own choices. I pretended to resume reading my newspaper and we sat together.

Todd Morgan's stories have appeared in *Split Lip Magazine* and *Every Day Fiction*. He was born in Indiana and grew up in Kentucky and New Jersey. He lives with his wife in Oak Park, Illinois.

BOOKSHELF BUILDER

FOR $38 (SHIPPED FREE), *SL*'S LAST FIVE ISSUES

Buy online under "Readers" at
www.sportliterate.org

Essay

Mrs. Talbot and a Field
Kent Jacobson

> *Life comes with indelible loss: lost innocence, lost loved ones, broken bonds, broken hearts, faulty choices . . . .*
>
> Bob Hohler

I remember a woman crossing her lawn, the doctor's wife, Mrs. Talbot, a slim woman in a dark faded shirtwaist, striding with this-is-my-world certainty, chin out, spine straight. She'd shot from her weathered-shingle second home on Winnapaug salt pond — the sharp smell, the squawking gulls, the jays, the blackbirds, low-hanging limbs heavy with apples. I was 12.

We played baseball in the summer twilight on Mrs. Talbot's field with its chicken-wired backstop and dirt bases, the sloping left field and the too deep right. Nobody ever hit a home run to right. Nobody. One kid was the son of a double-amputee chicken farmer, and another, the son of his foreman. A third was a string bean with a future in basketball; his dad sold insurance. Another's cousin would play in the baseball All-Star game, his father a state trooper. My nearest neighbors and buddies — the Crandalls and the Smiths — came from families where mom and dad worked the factory lines. And me, I was the kid who lived on the lone hill, Mom at the University, Dad head of the state forest service. We boys were a mixed collection, just enough of us, we always said, "for a decent game."

We scrapped and recited. "Who forgot the first baseman's glove?" "Get the damn ball over the plate. Arm needs a tune-up." "Where's the good bat?" "You didn't tag 'im, you didn't tag 'im." "Overthrow first and you go find it in the high grass." We were that kind of family. Each night we bickered for the good of the game. Ball fired to the plate, crack of a bat against beat-up ball, "In the air, in the air, Go back, go back," runner streaks, "Second, he's at second," ball in Mike Smith's glove in left and a bad throw to third, ball wide, runner scores, "Missed a base, he missed a base." The game was like a song shout with Chuck Berry and the Yankees' World War II marine outfielder Hank Bauer, revered for grit and a face "like a clenched fist."

I was different from the other boys, Mrs. Talbot's permission said. I was special. I could be trusted. They couldn't. I was flattered.

But then there was Mrs. Talbot. She had an underground, fresh-water spring that poured cold into the marsh, steps from her shingled home. In the August heat, t-shirts sopped, jeans stuck to our thighs, we threw our gloves down to hold our spot and howled across her lawn like we owned the place, the salt smell sharper, and gulped at her spring, the water clean, the water clear... and whooped our way back past the lilac and summersweet, the rhododendron and hydrangea, back over her green wide lush lawn to our field.

Mrs. Talbot complained. She said we were too many. There was noise. We wore a path. No water, she said, no more use of the spring.

What'd she say?

We weren't certain the verdict was final. It couldn't be. Adults said piles of things, much of which we tried to ignore.

I headed for the spring. That's when Mrs. T appeared, that stride. I froze.

Adults talked to kids when we needed a correction and I sensed mine was coming now.

She spoke in a whisper without a hint of hesitation. "It's alright if *you* come here for water. I won't allow anyone else."

Wha . . .?

The boys could see us. I should have gone back to the field right then, told them, Forget it. Verdict's final. She's serious. No water.

Mrs. Talbot retreated to the house. I stood there. I watched her go. I turned for the spring.

Why? Why did I do that? Why wasn't I wiser?

Mrs. T, I thought, is looking after me. She's singled me out. One boy's okay. I'm not the army of the 11 of us. I'm quiet, though how does she know?

And sure, my older sister was smart and Mrs. Talbot's sister, my new English teacher for the college-bound, gave A's to my soaked-in-books sister. That counted for something. Mrs. Talbot and my family were nearest neighbors (even if we didn't speak), us up on the hill, 25 rooms, a stone porch and fountain, Japanese maples and an ocean view. On nights and weekends Dad and Mom had transformed a three-story derelict mansion into a summer inn (Winnapaug House) to pay for sis' and my college.

I was different from the other boys, Mrs. Talbot's permission said. I was special. I could be trusted. They couldn't. I was flattered.

I swallowed the message whole.

I must have told the boys, though I can't remember. I don't want to remember. No water except for me. Did I appear smug and pleased?

No one protested, not openly.

Their dads may have said: Live with it. He isn't like us. He's like Mrs. Talbot. Though some boys had to balk: Why him? What's wrong with me? He's just a kid like us.

All the boys would slip from my life and never see me as older men except that time on a New Haven train when Randy and Kenny Crandall passed and didn't speak. We didn't forget, none of us could forget, because we'd had a glimpse early of the way the world would likely work.

You can betray your friends and simultaneously betray who you are and who you have been, and spend much of your life from that point on finding your way back, all the way back… to one isolated abandoned field off the main road.

Kent Jacobson has been a filmmaker, foundation executive, and college teacher. His writing appears (or will soon appear) in *The Dewdrop*, *Hobart*, *Backchannels*, *Talking Writing*, *Punctuate*, *Bull*, and elsewhere. He lives with his wife, landscape architect Martha Lyon, in Massachusetts, two hours from Mrs. Talbot's field.

S**Literate**

BUILT FOR ANY BUDGET

SPORT LITERATE REMAINS $20 FOR TWO ISSUES
CONSIDER BULKING UP WITH TWO SUBSCRIPTIONS FOR
YOURSELF AND A WORKOUT BUDDY

Subscribe online:
www.sportliterate.org

Poetry

Referred Pain
Leland Seese

"Referred pain is when the pain you feel in one part of your body is actually caused by pain or injury in another part of your body." (Healthline website)

A frying pan held too long above a fire,
he crossed the infield spitting, ticking,
Give the goddam ball to me!
I thought I did it right,
first baseman in a pick-off drill,
high school baseball practice.
He was going Lou Piniella on me —
Piniella, screaming in the ump's face
before he throws the first base bag
clear to centerfield.
He was never gonna be a Lou Piniella and,
truth be told, I was no true ballplayer.
Now he pushed his bristled, jowly face
inches from my eyes, unblinking.
*What the hell you think
you're doing anyway?*
An existential question
for a boy of seventeen.
I turned and started running
for the lake, to wash away
my coach's pain.

Leland Seese will always treasure his tenth year of life in 1969, when he followed his hometown team, the Seattle Pilots, on KVI every day, and sat in Sick's Stadium a dozen times or more to see them in person. His poems appear in *Sport Literate, The Christian Century, The Chestnut Review,* and many other journals. And his debut chapbook, *Wherever This All Ends* (Kelsay Books), opens, closes, and hinges on three baseball poems.

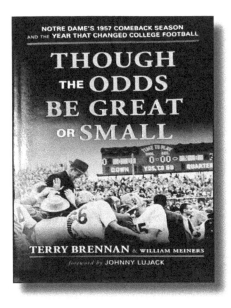

Co-authored by Terry Brennan and *Sport Literate*'s own William Meiners, *Though the Odds Be Great or Small* is the "undertold story" of Notre Dame's 1957 football season. And you can read about it during the 65th anniversary of that season.

From the fleet-footed little brother on some of the Irish's greatest teams in the 1940s to the young coach (hired at 25), Brennan weathered a 2-8 season in 1956 with limited scholarship players. The comeback campaign in 1957 (7-3) was highlighted with a shutout win on the road against mighty Oklahoma.

GET A SIGNED COPY

FOR $21.99 (INCLUDES SHIPPING AND HANDLING)

ALL PROCEEDS GO BACK TO *SPORT LITERATE*

Buy online:
www.sportliterate.org

Essay

Swearing in the Suburbs
Jason Koo

I remember the day I first learned to swear. In Maumee, Ohio, a suburb of Toledo, where I lived from kindergarten through third grade.

Mommy, Ohio. We lived on Wyandotte Road. My porn name — the name of my first pet plus the street I grew up on — is Romeo Wyandotte. Up and down the long, winding streets of Mommy's neighborhood, young Romeo Wyandotte went wobbling as he learned how to bike, spitting at the wind when it made him fall over. Spitting because he didn't yet know how to swear.

My best friend Jay, the one who taught me how, lived next door. He was a cherubic, dimpled blonde kid who moved into the neighborhood when I was entering the third grade, just a year before my family moved to another suburb, the famous Shaker Heights of Cleveland. I don't know how we became best friends; I think one day he just rang our doorbell and said he'd moved in next door, did I want to play? Friendships were so easy back then; all the kids on my street played with each other and went to each other's houses. The day my mom took me to buy my first bike, a brown BMX with yellow padding and handlebars, all my friends cheered and chased after our station wagon on their bikes like some scene out of Steven Spielberg.

Jay and I did everything together, perhaps influenced by the similarity of our names. Both our parents kept pointing this out to us, as if they thought it was the most hilarious thing in the world (my parents called me "Jay" for short, except when they were mad). Jay slept over at my place; I slept over at his. His family once took me to watch one of his Little League games, the second baseball game I ever watched (the first was in Korea). I watched him strike out like 10 times. His sister, also blonde, whom I always remember wearing a fuzzy white cardigan, gently explained that he was having a bad game. His older brother gave me some grape-flavored Big League Chew, which I thought was the most amazing thing I'd ever tasted.

Jay's older brother also taught me how to attach a playing card to my bike so that the rear wheel would make a ticking sound as I rode. No doubt it was making that sound on the day I learned to swear. I don't know how exactly it happened; I was hanging out with Jay, his sister and his brother, and one of them, probably Jay, who was the youngest and most daring, introduced me to words like *shit, fuck, son of a bitch, asshole, motherfucker.* I remember riding my bike with them, gleefully shouting those words at Jay as he sped away from me: *I'm gonna get you, you son of a bitch! You asshole! You motherfucker!* The words felt incredible in my mouth. His sister was laughing and ducking her head a little, saying, Shhh! I kept swearing in the sun, released into a new country of language, Jay biking away faster and faster, trying to get as far away from the scene of the verbal crime as possible.

After that, I swore all the time — except around my parents, obviously. The first time I got caught was when my older sister and I put on some kind of carnival for the other kids in our backyard — we did this sort of thing — which included a clown act starring Jay and me. I remember rolling around on the lawn with him in our wigs and makeup, pillows fattening our shirts — I think this was the fight scene? — muttering, *You son of a bitch, I'll kill you, you son of a bitch.* I seemed to like *son of a bitch* the most, at least in my recollection, which is funny since I never say that now, despite using just about every other permutation of swearing known to man (*fucknut, sonofafuckingfucknut,* etc.). My mom missed this, but my sister told on me, saying I'd said some bad words and other people — parents included — could hear me. I thought I was just whispering these things to Jay, but he too said afterward that I was saying this shit really loud.

Can't remember what my punishment was, but somehow I wasn't forbidden to hang out with Jay, whom I must have blamed for the bad words. One day I was kicking around a soccer ball with Jay and his older brother on their front lawn and noticed how different our families were. For some reason Jay decided to kick the ball in the direction of his house, and he kicked it so hard it fucking *shattered* the living room window. His mom, freaked, came screaming out the front door, looking for blood. At first she went after the older brother, but he kindly stepped aside, redirecting her fury toward Jay like a matador maneuvering a bull. She told him to *get the fuck over here* and pulled him by his blonde hair into the house.

I'd never seen a parent do or say anything like that before. That just didn't happen in Mommy, Ohio. It was a little scary, but I wanted to know what happened in that house after Jay went inside. It looked like his mom was going to do to his head what the soccer ball did to that window.

But the next time I saw him, he acted like nothing had happened. Which was a little disappointing. He looked the same, too.

The next year we moved to Shaker Heights and I never saw Jay again, this All-American blonde kid who gave me the gift of swearing. The irony about that last image I have of him is that he was the more well-behaved one between the two of us; his parents assumed I was good, probably because I was Asian. In fact I remember Jay bizarrely trying to blame the soccer ball incident on me as he went into the house sobbing, as if I'd put him up to it, saying, *But Jason* (insert crying-muffled words here)…

Did I put him up to it? Maybe my swearing was enough to pin the blame on me. Maybe I'd built up so much aggression in him that he had to release it by kicking a soccer ball through a window. Here he was thinking he'd teach this nice Asian kid some bad words, maybe just for kicks, maybe to help me be cool, and then this kid turns into a swearing motherfucking *beast*.

Swearing for me has always been about asserting my identity out of the realm of control. At least that's my rationalization for enjoying something that so many other people find distasteful. I don't just like swearing; I *love* swearing. If you could hear me at home swearing to myself, or more accurately at my internet connection speed or Time Warner cable bill, you might be amused; if you could hear me swearing in my car at the *motherfucking-fuckwads* I do battle with on the streets of NYC, you'd never get into a car with me; if you could hear me swearing when watching Cleveland baseball games alone, you'd probably recommend I seek professional help. And I don't just swear in private. I swear in my poems, I swear in my prose (as you are now well aware), I swear while teaching, I swear on social media. My Twitter erupts into a fuckstorm of swearing with every baseball game I watch; usually by the end of the game I've lost at least four or five followers. I can be swept with joy — "HOLY SHIT NICK MOTHERFUCKING SWISHER!!!!!" (Jun 19, 2014: Nick Swisher's utterly improbable walk-off grand slam) — or crushing keys in rage — "John Axford, pardon my French, but you are a fucking piece of shit" (Jun 20, 2014: John Axford 8th-inning collapse) — the language is the same. My mom keeps telling me to stop swearing on Twitter, but I can't help it — that's me.

Swearing was probably an unconscious pleasure at first, as I'd always lived in a controlled environment; bad words must have felt like a fun way to disrupt that. But as I've matured (which is debatable) and caught on to how Asians and Asian Americans are perceived, i.e. controlled, as model minorities in this country, it's become a more conscious pleasure. I like seeing how people's perceptions of me change when I open my mouth, especially when I read my poems. There's always an uncomfortable silence or laughter or both when I read the opening lines of "Model Minority":

I was thinking on the subway yesterday and thinking I think this fairly
Frequently, *Fuhhhck* these people…

This is far from the haiku or haiku-like poetry most people expect of me or perhaps wish I'd write instead, especially when they hear my last name contained in the sound haiku ("Hi Koo"). Sometimes I almost wish I could

When we moved to Shaker Heights, I discovered Cleveland sports and my life in swearing began in earnest.

give it to them, this elegant Eastern mystical chrysanthemum mumbo jumbo they want, because hey, I like that shit too when I'm in the right mood, and I don't want to be remembered only as the guy who drops f-bombs in his poetry, especially if the takeaway is that I'm amusing and outrageous, i.e. a circus freak (Caliban), but not a "real" poet, i.e. someone who doesn't have to drop f-bombs in his poetry to get people's attention (Prospero). I have plenty of poems that don't swear, but my most well-known poems are probably "Morning, Motherfucker," "Model Minority," and "Swearing by Effingham," the first poem in my first book, which begins,

> Effingham, IL, let's just let it all out.
>   Sometimes you need to call a fucking ham
> a fucking ham.

I deliberated over placing this poem first in my first book because of the stamp that double "fucking" would put on my poems right from the start. I didn't want to make people think I relied on that kind of language for effect or turn them off after just three lines. But ultimately I went with it because I saw I wasn't just swearing in the sense of saying bad words; I was *swearing an oath* to my kind of language, a "ham" (hard as a motherfucker) sensibility, if that doesn't sound too ridiculous. I was swearing *by* swearing, placing my faith in it. Swearing not to restrain myself from *fucking* out of a sense of decorum, the decorum I'd grown up with and come to find was expected of me as an Asian American. Swearing to let a language out that was appropriate to how I felt rather than simply appropriate. Swearing not to sound like a model minority.

When we moved to Shaker Heights, I discovered Cleveland sports and my life in swearing began in earnest. Actually I may never have gotten into sports had it not been for the New York Mets and their miraculous 1986 World Series victory over the Boston Red Sox. My parents explained when we moved that one of the fun parts of being in Cleveland was that I could watch the Browns and Tribe and Cavs but also root for New York teams, since I was born in New York.

(This was bullshit, but it sounded right at the time.) So when all my friends in the fifth grade talked on the bus about how they were rooting for the Red Sox, I said I was rooting for the Mets. I loved Keith Hernandez and Lenny Dykstra and Wally Backman and Jesse Orosco and Darryl Strawberry and Gary Carter. What names! What handlebar mustaches! Lamentably, I missed the Bill Buckner game — we were at a family friend's house celebrating something that obviously was *not* important, in retrospect — but I watched the Game 7 comeback, in which my hero, "Keithy," delivered a clutch hit, and so the first time I rooted for a team, that team won it all.

That has not been my experience of the world since. Later that fall, I started watching the Browns, who had the whole city in their thrall by going a magical 12–4 behind our apparent white savior, Bernie Kosar. They sealed my fate for good as a *Cleveland* fan, not a New York fan, when they came back to beat the Jets in double overtime in the first round of the playoffs, miraculously tying the game in regulation after going down 10 with only 4:14 remaining. But they crushed me in the AFC Championship game. Bernie and Brian Brennan got us to the brink of the Super Bowl with a go-ahead touchdown bomb within the final six minutes that had my dad and me jumping up and down yelling in front of the television blocking the view of my mom and two sisters —

And then the Drive happened.

Still, how could I not fall in love with Cleveland sports through Bernie Kosar and Webster Slaughter and Ozzie Newsome and Hanford Dixon and Frank Minnifield and the Dawg Pound? (Were names just cooler in the '80s?) The Dawg Pound was awesome, the little dog bones and batteries people threw into the end zone, plunking John Elway on the helmet, dog masks, *woof woof woof,* plastic headsets that speared your head with a bone. I'd never seen anything like that in Maumee and wanted to be a part of it.

Sports, like swearing, was a liberating new language that took me out of the sameness of the suburbs into more visceral, violent country, where pain was possible. I liked the community of people I felt through sports: raw, passionate motherfuckers who didn't give a damn about the decorum I was taught at home. I wanted to be in the Dawg Pound, stirring shit up. Instead I was taking tennis lessons at the Mayfield Racquet Club — my mom was driving us to a tennis lesson as Elway led the Drive, which in retrospect saved me some televisual trauma, though Nev Chandler's radio play-by-play is still burned into my brain — and trying to catch the game on TV during water breaks, or at home on the brown living room carpet next to my mom and dad, who didn't get *into* it enough, in my opinion. I wanted to go crazy, releasing my emotions; swearing was the only proportional response to what was happening on the field. But my mom and dad were always monitoring my activity. At first they encouraged my getting into sports, but once they saw how crazy I got while watching the games they tried to corral my obsession, reminding me that whatever I was watching was *just a game.*

This has always been a phrase I've loathed. It was obviously more than just a game. What we were talking about was nothing less than my gateway into life.

Watching football was fine, because it was only on once a week and the whole family watched the game together; but baseball was another story. There was a game on almost every day. And I had to watch or listen to every game. If I didn't follow every game, then the next one didn't mean as much; each game was a new chapter in the story the season was writing. My first full season of watching Cleveland baseball came in 1987, when our team was picked by *Sports Illustrated* to win the World Series after 38 years of futility (they hadn't won since 1948). They proceeded to lose 102 games. I watched or listened to almost every one. This, remember, was in the days before MLB.com, when you couldn't watch or listen to every game easily through your computer or phone; many games were not even televised. So I had to make a concerted daily effort to subject myself to all this losing. I'd tune in to listen to Herb Score call the game on my alarm clock radio while doing my homework, keeping the volume low so my mom couldn't hear and staying at the ready to turn the radio off if I heard her steps outside my door. I tried to watch the game on TV whenever I could — actual images of the action were heaven — but this wasn't often, because even if the game was on TV, turning it on meant signaling to my mom what I was doing.

The irony — isn't there always a fucking irony? — about my getting into sports and swearing is that I got into them for the feeling of community they offered and ended up feeling lonelier and more insane. No one else among my family and friends has ever been as obsessed about Cleveland baseball as I am. Following games on the sly as a kid meant I couldn't erupt as I wanted to in response to what was happening (usually bad), so my experience of baseball became painfully interiorized; the games were so personal that I began taking them too personally. If I'd had anything like a Dawg Pound of like-minded souls available to back me in swearing my fucking mouth off any time the team did something terrible, I may have grown into a more "normal" sports fan and maybe wouldn't swear so much now.

I went through some shit in Missouri, which you can read about in my first book — or just imagine, as it's not hard to imagine (this is *Missouri* we're talking about) — and the only way I was going to convey this was by saying *shit* to describe the shit, calling a fucking ham a *fucking ham.* I'd pass Effingham, Illinois, on my drive home to Cleveland for the holidays, thinking about all the shit I was going through and how "Effingham" couldn't harbor how I felt. The name was amusing, as was imagining what went on there, what kind of language people used, but I had to get past the amusing in my poetry (a "problem" at the time) in order to pierce through to the actual reality of my life. I may have lived in Effingham before, but now I was most definitely in Fuckingham:

> Effingham, I salute the muffling
> of your name, the comic elegance
>
> of so much restraint, as if you were slipping
> onto the punches of tongues large aqua-blue mittens;
> in an earlier life I may have enjoyed
> a certain camaraderie in your bleachers,
>
> booing your effing quarterback fumbling
> the effing snap, or asking what a man has to do
> to get some effing fries up in this place;
> but now I need a city to carry the rawer
>
> sound in my chest, the hate concocting
> a whole new slew of vowels, where to unleash
> such words as I mull might not bruise
> other ears but be gratifying and returned
>
> with thanks.

But of course no matter how rude my language became, I was still writing poetry; I wasn't *just* saying "shit" to describe the shit. Poetry, no matter how direct, is never direct; there's always a little detour it takes you through.

Why write poetry then? Poetry was an unlikely third language I took on after swearing and sports because of the even more alluring sense of community it offered than they did. But together with the other two, it (yes, ironically) ended up making me feel triply lonely and insane.

I didn't have poetry in my life growing up, aside from what I read in school. My parents were immigrants from South Korea still learning English during my early years, and while they always stressed the importance of reading, I don't remember them ever reading poetry out loud to me when I was a kid or putting a book of poetry into my hands, in English or Korean. Some poets talk about reading and writing poetry since childhood or absorbing it as an unconscious influence through their parents reading to them — that was not me. My becoming a poet was about as improbable as me becoming a professional baseball player, based on how I was raised — in fact, more so, because baseball at least I started following and playing in the fifth grade. Poetry I didn't really discover until late in high school; and, true to form, the discovery was indirect and took years to unfold.

The verbal score I got when I first started practicing for the PSAT in middle school was appallingly low, something like 330 — certainly not an early indicator that I could get into an Ivy League school, as my parents wanted, let alone become a poet. The low score was unsurprising, because I had no interest in reading or writing; my parents never really pushed me to read for pleasure (rather than just for school) or excel at writing the way they pushed me in math; my mom drilled my older sister and me in times tables late into the night at the kitchen table when we were in elementary school. Alarmed, my mom tried to address this deficiency the only way she knew how: by making me study SAT vocabulary flashcards — plethora, indefatigable, modicum — and do practice tests over and over again. Any time I was free and wanted to catch a ball game, she'd scold me by saying I should be practicing for the SAT. After about a year of this, I raised my verbal score enough to qualify for admission to the John Hopkins Center for Talented Youth summer programs, where after first enrolling me in courses in math and chemistry, my mom eventually signed me up for writing courses, as that verbal score stubbornly refused to come up to Ivy League level.

I noticed an immediate difference about the writing courses: they had girls in them. The math and chemistry courses were almost all boys, resulting in me being bored out of my fucking mind as I sat in these classrooms during the summers when I turned 14 (1990) and 15 (1991), especially as I switched to an all-boys private school at the start of my high school years. But "Writing and Society" with Pat Conners, which I took at the Franklin & Marshall campus in Lancaster, Pennsylvania, during the second session of the summer program of '91, had a decidedly different vibe. Vicky Chen, Marilyn Fu, Minah Kim — this warm, attractive, outgoing and obviously smart triumvirate of Asian girls immediately took an interest in me when we met and tried to draw me out of my shell. They showed me I *had* a shell. I remember how enthusiastically, almost aggressively, they tried to befriend me in the first few days outside of class, literally calling me out of my dorm room to come hang out with them; I was flattered but also embarrassed. Finally, one night, I agreed, as Minah (the Korean one) wouldn't take no for an answer. I came outside and had no idea what to do with myself, especially my arms and hands — what did one do with these things when standing around trying to talk to girls? Vicky disappeared into her dorm and reemerged a few minutes later on the balcony above, wearing a new tank top. The tank top she had on before was a perfectly attractive piece of clothing, so even my clueless, unversed dork of a self was able to read this as a sign of interest. But instead of staying to talk to her when she came back down, I ducked back into my dorm room.

I spent the rest of that summer and, in some ways, the rest of my high school years mourning my decision not to stay out there. The girls gave up on me after that, though they were still nice to me, and instead of possibly enjoying (and learning from) the first romance of my life with Vicky, I nursed a crush on her that I didn't do anything about until the last night of the session when, towards the end of one of the famed CTY dances (which always end with "American Pie"), I asked her to slow dance, probably to "Forever Young" (this conjecture is based on my adult affection for a song I couldn't stand when I was actually young). And then we shared a couple of long hugs the next day when I was leaving and promised to write to each other — which we did over the next year or so, as did Marilyn and I, though predictably the letters petered out and eventually stopped coming as we entered our last two years of high school. Vicky and Marilyn both handwrote their letters and did this magical thing where they'd package them in envelopes they created out of magazine pages, giving them an extra personal, feminine touch; I typed my letters and sent them in business envelopes until, schooled by them, I took up their approach.

Thus writing, which I used to struggle at and hate, quickly became a new interest of mine when I realized it was a gateway to girls like Vicky, Marilyn, and Minah and the wider world of fun, culture, and sociality they represented. In this regard, writing was even superior to swearing and sports, my two loves. I gained a confidence over the three weeks of "Writing and Society" that transformed me from the guy hiding in his dorm room to the one asking Vicky to slow dance, which might not seem like much but to me at the time was huge; people *responded* to the things I wrote in class in a way that carried a social cachet I hadn't felt before. Which is to say they responded to *me*, as an identity, an individual with ideas and wit and imagination. I remember after the first thing I shared, Gunny Scarfo (who would go on to become my best friend) let out a loud, slow *YeaahhHHH* and led the class in applause, which surprised me, because I didn't think the thing was any good (I don't remember what I wrote at all, which tells me it was terrible). No one responded like this to me, or anyone, in a math or science class; one's identity was not part of the equation of success there, only one's abstract powers of cognition. I didn't feel *seen*, with a body, a face, a life story — I was simply wrong or right. And, being Asian, I was expected to be right, just like all the other Asians. So excelling meant merely being part of the faceless horde of replicating Asian math machines.

With writing, I could actually be bad and still be seen. I certainly wasn't a "good" writer in "Writing and Society"; I had no real idea what I was doing (which is why my mom had signed me up for the class in the first place) and still didn't enjoy reading and would tune out in class for long stretches. Notably, when Pat Connors spent one class teaching us iambic pentameter out of the blue, this dormant poet spaced out so badly that when it came time to try writing in the meter ourselves, he panicked and started asking everyone around him for help. I could not comprehend what we were being asked to do — we had to do *what*? Count syllables? *Why*? Was I back in math class?!

I cared more for the response to my writing than for writing itself, seeking to entertain. I penned a long horror story named "C.L.O.S.E.T." (those periods might lead you to believe the title was an acronym for something, but you would be wrong), hoping to impress the guys in my dorm, who loved Stephen King; I shared the story during one of the Friday-night sleepovers in the common room and Vic, one of our RAs, was impressed enough that he asked if he could share it during the campus open mic the next afternoon.

I enjoyed this nascent feeling that some people saw me as a writer, even though I knew it was a pose. I started reading a lot of Stephen King — the first contemporary writer I read on my own — to try to fit the pose, tackling his biggest books like *The Stand* and *It* to prove I was legit. But so-called "serious" literature was still Greek to me, especially the shit originally written in Greek. I don't recall a single book I read in English class my sophomore year of high school, which shows how much that stuff stuck. But the following summer I persuaded my mom to enroll me in "The Craft of Fiction" at the CTY campus in Carlisle, Pennsylvania, where Gunny planned to take the same course. This was my chance to get real.

This was also the summer I was determined to be cool. I hadn't felt "cool" in a long time — not since the fifth grade. But this summer, I'd have Gunny beside me (who's always had the gift of making everyone he talks to feel they're special at something, even people who seem decidedly unspecial to everyone else) and I'd be in a class where there were sure to be a lot of girls and I could wow them with my writing talents. And there were indeed girls — no mythical Asian American triumvirate this time, but white girls experienced in creative writing from their schools who hung out with the cool white kids on campus, the ones who'd sit in charmed acoustic-guitar circles and sing classic folk songs on the quad over the weekend. They were friendly to me and affirmed what I was doing, and I became close with one of them, Lindsay, who'd sit next to me in class and scrawl notes into my notebook (usually gossip about other students or our teacher) and later became my main pen pal, taking up the void left by Vicky and Marilyn during my last two years of high school. She introduced me to the Grateful Dead by sending me a great mix tape and even managed to visit me once during my senior year (not sure how I convinced my mom to agree to this) so that we could go to a Grateful Dead concert (which we did in secret, as obviously there was no way my mom would agree to this).

Nothing romantic ever developed between us, though. I only had eyes for one girl that summer: Cara, a cool blonde girl from Virginia who seemed older and more glamorous than everyone else. The first time I saw her, on the first Friday night of the session, she was dressed like a rock star, wearing a revealing black mesh top and ripped jeans. She kept walking back and forth across the quad alone, as if she were looking for somebody; I found it hard to believe she hadn't already manifested a boyfriend. Determined not to repeat my mistake with Vicky, I forced myself to go up to her and introduce myself at the end of the night. That went like this: Hi! I just wanted to meet you. Then after names and a few words, I ran away.

Trying to be cool, I hadn't yet convinced myself I was cool enough; I didn't believe I could sustain the interest of someone like Cara. Later I understood that she wasn't looking *for* somebody that night; she was looking to *meet* somebody — that's why she kept walking back and forth. I think I was the only guy who approached her (possibly because everyone, guys and girls, was intimidated by her looks), and she seemed eager, almost relieved, when I stopped her and said I wanted to meet her. If I hadn't been so awkward during that first conversation, effectively preventing it from *being* a conversation, I might've become the person she was looking to meet.

Instead I became the person who dogged her that summer, joining her and her roommate Natasha at every meal and trying to be interesting in conversation and persistently failing. I got a sense of how much I'd annoyed Natasha when she wrote, "Try to have a DAY," in the journal I passed around at the end of the session to get people's mementos and addresses. I'd somehow developed the notion that I could be "cool" to girls by being negative about everything, which went hand in hand with acting like I knew something about everything. Cara was taking "The Craft of Poetry," and when she told me this I announced, "I hate poetry." I think I was trying to demonstrate that *I* was a fiction writer, explaining everything that was wrong about poetry as a genre, how you couldn't understand what the fuck poets were saying and what was the fucking point of that? But obviously this was just about the dumbest fucking thing I could've said to a girl interested in poetry whom I was trying to get interested in me.

Cara was always unfailingly polite, so she didn't argue with me or stop talking to me; she just kindly countered that, yeah, sometimes poetry was hard to understand but she liked it anyway. I saw her one day during a class break sitting on top of a low wall with a pen in hand and a notebook on her lap — her class was writing outside. I went up to her and asked her what she was doing and she said, deflated, "Trying to be inspired." She looked as though she felt she weren't interesting enough to write a good poem, and I tried to encourage her, because of course at the time I thought she was the most interesting person on the planet. This seemed to cheer her up, and I remember this as the best conversation we had. She started to open up to me, probably because I wasn't so determined to act cool (like a jackass).

This was, I think, when my turn toward poetry began. I didn't know it at the time, but something about Cara's quiet resistance to my declaration "I hate poetry" and the vulnerability of her longing to be inspired, to be something other than herself, drew me in as a possible home. I was drawn to swearing and then sports because of the sense they offered of something authentic *beyond* the life I was living in suburban Ohio, which felt fabricated, isolated. But swearing and sports fandom didn't lead to girls; writing did. And writing *poetry* led to someone like Cara, for whom pose didn't work. There was a dignity to her relationship to poetry that gave my attempts to be cool through writing — to be somebody — the lie.

Poetry was a beyond that required a greater commitment to access. Two years later, as I started my freshman year of college at Yale (my mom's investment in CTY courses had paid off), I was very much in the opposite camp to "I hate poetry." I was writing poems on my own and, more importantly, reading poems on my own outside of the "Major English Poets" we were asked to read for the English major. That was the year I discovered Hart Crane, Elizabeth Bishop, John Ashbery, Rainer Maria Rilke, and rediscovered poets like Blake, Keats and Whitman whom I'd been bored by in high school, back when I hated poetry. The poems I was writing were terrible — a quasi-lyrical amalgam of all these poets crossed with Steve Malkmus of Pavement — but they caught the interest of Tania, another seemingly unattainable blonde like Cara, who, inexplicably, left her boyfriend for awkward, acne'd me, citing my writing her poems as a big reason why. I was still more poseur than poet, but at least I wasn't saying I hated something I knew nothing about to impress her (well, except Frank O'Hara's poetry, because her boyfriend said he liked it), and I was actually *reading* poetry, and some pretty damn difficult stuff at that. I'd succeeded in becoming more authentically a somebody through poetry than I had been when I met Cara.

The more I got into poetry, though, the more relentless I became about trying to leave that poseur self behind, which, at a place like Yale, meant conquering a vast white canon of authors it never would have occurred to me to read or take seriously before. Harold Bloom's *The Western Canon* came out the year I entered college, and it provided a daunting roadmap to all I didn't know, a kind of syllabus to a course on "How to Be a Major Poet" that effectively took all of my undergrad years and then my MFA and PhD years after that to (start to) complete. The influence of that book, and Bloom himself as a professor, and John Hollander, who even more than Bloom was like an incarnation of all the knowledge the book indicated one had to have to be taken seriously, living proof that it was actually possible for a poet to have read that much, so I couldn't just blow Bloom off — this is why I lived alone my junior year of college, so I could read without distraction, as I took courses on writers not even my most bookish friends were interested in, such as Ben Jonson and Fernando Pessoa. That Pessoa course, ironically titled "Pessoa & Co.," consisted of me and one other student, a grad student studying Portuguese literature. The professor said the course wouldn't run if I didn't take it. This only inflated my sense of the importance of what I was doing.

You've probably guessed that Tania and I broke up before that year. I was responding to a calling, I felt, but rather than becoming more heroic or spiritual or self-possessed, I just grew weirder and weirder, alienating myself from Tania and any human company at all. I had to block out absurdly huge chunks of time for reading every day, to catch up on all the stuff I hadn't read before (when I'd wasted my childhood), and this meant I barely saw the few friends I'd made my first two years of college and, when I went home, barely spoke to my family except at meals. About the only other thing I still made time for was baseball, as the Cleveland club went through a golden age during my college years, making the playoffs every fall and the World Series twice, in '95 and '97. But this only alienated me further, as I was surrounded by Yankees and Red Sox fans in the Northeast, and Cleveland came up short both times they went to the Series, losing in particularly devastating fashion to the Marlins in '97 when Jose Mesa couldn't hold a 2–1 lead in the ninth. I didn't speak to anyone for days after that, shutting myself in my room and replaying every fatal mistake Mesa made in my head, trying to convince myself he didn't really blow it, watching *The Natural* and *Major League* at night to try to comfort myself with Hollywood endings.

To this day, I still can't watch the ending of *Major League* without crying (I literally just watched it again on YouTube before writing this, and cried), when Willie Mays Hayes dashes home all the way from second to score the winning run against the Yankees on a surprise bunt by aging catcher Jake Taylor, who'd just called his shot (twice), and the Cleveland crowd mobs the field in joy. I didn't cry when I watched the movie as a kid; I only started crying during these lonely college years. I think the tears started not because of the outcome — after all, we didn't win the World Series, just beat the Yankees in a one-game playoff to win the division[1] — but because of the image of joyful community I saw on the field, players and fans leaping in

---

1 Admittedly, "just" beating the Yankees in a one-game playoff is baseball fucking heaven, the second-best outcome to winning the World Series, which was one consolation to that '97 postseason: we'd beaten the Yankees in the ADLS by taking a winner-take-all Game 5 after coming back against the great Mariano Rivero to win Game 4 and tie the series 2-2.

delirium and embracing, all guards down, released into a transcendent togetherness. This was a feeling I'd always longed for, why I'd gotten into sports and poetry in the first place, but I found myself painfully distant from it the more I'd gotten into those things, especially in combination. It's hard to find fellowship when sports and poetry are the two main passions in your life, as usually people into sports are not into poetry and vice versa; it's even harder when you're passionate about *Cleveland* sports and most passionate about Cleveland *baseball*, and you express that passion in the form of indefatigable swearing, and the poetry you're most passionate about reading is the long, sprawling, difficult kind featuring a plethora of subjects and changes in diction and tone, and the poetry you most like to write is the long, sprawling, difficult kind featuring a plethora of subjects and changes in diction and tone including Cleveland sports and swearing. That's a pretty difficult combination for anyone to relate to, even the modicum of people who do happen to like both sports and poetry. Throw in the fact that I was a second-generation Korean American male, the only son of a physician, expected to become a physician himself, and that no book of poetry in English by a Korean American male had been published in America until 1998, the year I graduated from college, and you get the picture. I couldn't possibly see the whole picture at the time, but I remember having the eerie feeling while watching the Marlins' nauseating post-game celebration that this loss had determined my fate. I was at a crossroads earlier, a 21-year-old watching a mirror of himself in the 21-year-old rookie Jaret Wright pitching us to a 2–1 lead, thinking if we win this game, what will happen? What will that feel like? I felt that my makeup might fundamentally change, that I might lead a different life.

But we lost and that sealed it: I would be a poet. And I would be alone.

Jason Koo is a second-generation Korean American poet, educator, editor and nonprofit director. He is the author of three full-length collections of poetry: More Than Mere Light, America's Favorite Poem and Man on Extremely Small Island, winner of the De Novo Poetry Prize and the Asian American Writers' Workshop Members' Choice Award for the best Asian American book of 2009. His work has been published or is forthcoming in Best American Poetry 2022, the Missouri Review, Village Voice and Yale Review, among other places, and won fellowships from the National Endowment for the Arts, Vermont Studio Center and New York State Writers Institute. He is an associate teaching professor of English at Quinnipiac University and the founder and executive director of Brooklyn Poets.

Essay

Pitching Lessons
Bill Gruber

On the morning of September 20, 1964, the Philadelphia Phillies looked like heirs apparent to the National League pennant. With 12 games left to play in the season, manager Gene Mauch's team held a 6 ½ game lead over the St. Louis Cardinals and the Cincinnati Reds. Baseball commissioner Ford Frick gave the Phillies permission to print World Series tickets, and Jim Bunning, their pitching ace, appeared on the cover of *Sports Illustrated* as part of an article previewing the upcoming fall championships. Then, as sometimes happens in a vexatious world, the unthinkable occurred: the "fizz kids" lost the next 10 games in a row, and with them the pennant. It was a seismic upset; "the Phold," as the team's swoon came to be known, is still described on *Bleacher Report* as "the collapse by which all others are measured." Years later, when he was asked what he remembered about that September, Mauch, then managing the Minnesota Twins, muttered darkly, "Only every pitch."

The moment I read that story about Mauch, I knew that he and I were peas in a pod. True, I've never played professional baseball nor managed a major league team. But as the parent of a kid who was a baseball pitcher, I too know what it's like to live or die each time the ball starts its way toward home plate. In the spring of 1994, my six-year-old son Rob announced he wanted to play baseball for the local Baptist sports league in northeast Atlanta. At first, I was suspicious. Some years before, my daughter had attended a sleepover party for teens at the same church. After two hours in the company of an evangelistic youth group, for the first (and only) time ever, she called in my standing offer of a ride home from wherever she happened to be, no questions asked. The people who ran the baseball league, however, seemed genuinely to believe in the separation of church and sport. The tee-ball coach was Jewish, and the only commitment the Baptists sought was a registration fee.

That spring began what turned out to be 16 straight years watching my son play baseball, from tee-ball through travel teams, high school, and four years of pitching in college. It's been a trip, as they used to say, and now that it's over I want to set down some things I learned during the time I was the parent of an athlete. I don't claim to be an expert on things like player development, athletic scholarships, or regional showcases. As the father of a kid who never got recruitment solicitations from Division I baseball coaches, let alone professional scouts, I want to keep to simple, personal insights. What's it like to be the parent of a kid who pitched baseball?

In the first place, it gave me a new respect for high-school coaches, a class of people I once disdained. Now I know the difference good ones make. Blather all you want about leadership, respect for the sport, and motivational skills, or about qualities of character such as self-discipline or the willingness to accept responsibility for one's actions. The best coaches I saw brought something else to the table. Call it an instinct for words fitly spoken. They needn't be eloquent or couth.

It's February 4, 2002 — late afternoon, the first day of baseball tryouts at Chamblee High School in northeast Atlanta. I'm standing at the ball field with a gaggle of parents of eighth-grade JV hopefuls, bunched alongside a chain link fence set back from the third base line. Scudding clouds, thermometer nudging 40, a strong wind blowing in from right field. Not auspicious conditions for the sunshine game. Behind second and third base and at shortstop there's a line of kids. Three assistant coaches cluster around home plate, swatting ground balls to the stacked infielders; the kid at the front of the line fields the ball, or tries to, then throws over to first and rotates to the back. The whole drill moves along quickly, and nobody gets much individual attention; a couple of bobbles or errant throws and your baseball dream is over.

Fielding drills end just before five o'clock, when another line forms behind the pitcher's mound. Each pitching prospect throws to two batters — bigger kids, holdover team members from last year. I scrutinize the wannabe pitchers, but when it's Rob's turn, I walk away. I tell the person standing next to me that I don't want to be in my son's field of vision, but the truth is I'm too agitated to watch. When I return 10 minutes later, it's over. I spot my son headed toward the dugout. Walking with him is Coach D, head coach of varsity baseball; his arm is around Rob's shoulder. The coach is talking, but they're too far away to hear, and I can only guess at what he's saying. The individual attention seems a good sign, but you can never be sure. It might be a consolation speech — tough luck, kid, too many returning pitchers, hope to see you next year, yadda yadda yadda.

I'm surprised by the arm thing, though. I'm a teacher, and if I walked out of a class on Hamlet with my arm draped round a student there'd be stares and whispers. Rules for physical contact with coaches must be different, I assume — as were, I soon learned, those for speech. Driving home, I ask Rob for details. He repeats the coach's words, mimicking his Georgia drawl: "Son, you just saved your ass. Before you got on that mound, you were a cut bitch."

As we pull into the carport I'm still nonplussed. I tell my wife the whole story, including the conversation with the coach. She calls him a jerk and threatens to report him to the school board. By now I'm finding the speech more funny than offensive, and I meekly stick up for the coach. Maybe, I say, this is how you talk to cut through the hormonal fog of adolescent boys' brains? While we're arguing about sexist language and whether to complain to the school, Rob says he thought the coach had been supportive. My son seems happy and inspired, and we let the thing drop. The next year Coach D took a job coaching football at a much larger, 5-A high school; he never again had any direct interaction with my son, who played JV ball that season. Yet five years later, when Rob makes his college baseball team as a walk-on pitcher, he remembers that February afternoon and that loopy conversation, and he phones Coach D to thank him.

The second thing I learned is that American high schools force athletes to play a zero-sum game between sports and academics. Whenever players get caught in conflicts between the two, it's not necessarily their fault.

One week after tryouts I stood outside a classroom door at Chamblee Middle School, holding my son's bag of baseball gear. I was waiting to drive him to practice. The baseball field at the high school was five miles distant, and Rob was late. He was sitting in the room finishing up a math placement test. The exam was given each spring to all rising ninth-grade students to determine whether they qualified for a sequence of advanced math courses next year in high school. Administrators at the middle school had scheduled the math exam without thinking to see whether any kids had overlaps with after-school activities that were held off campus.

Rob had already missed the bus that shuttled students to the high school for sports and music, and I hovered just outside the classroom door with his gear, ready to rush him to the baseball field. The door was cracked open, and every few minutes I peeked inside to see if the test was wrapping up. I tried to make myself visible to my son while remaining beyond the sight of the math teacher who was proctoring the exam. She'd come up that afternoon from the high school where she was head of the math department and had acquired the status of a legend.

Dr. F (she had a Ph.D.) was striking — piercing eyes, gunmetal gray hair, fastidiously dressed. Depending on which rumor about her background you happened to hear, she was once a professional model, a stage actor, or the child of eastern European aristocrats displaced by the chaos of World War II. Also depending on your source of gossip, her age was somewhere between 52 and 86. After the fourth or fifth peek, Dr. F spotted me and headed my way. Her speech was formal. I thought I could detect the trace of an accent, possibly Slavic. Maybe the rumor about the aristocracy was true?

"Are you waiting for your child?"

Baseball has a reputation for being a lazy sport — the late sportswriter Pete Axthelm once called it "leisurely and pastoral" — but most events on a baseball field take place at the absolute limit of human physiological capabilities.

Instantly I was in one of those unexpected crises of parenting. I knew that this person had a formidable reputation in the school, and I knew about the great influence she had on kids' lives. I knew my son was smart, and I wanted her to think well of him. For that matter, I wanted her to think well of me, too. I knew my son loved math. I knew that one of the most important things any parent can pass on to a child is respect for learning. I knew that in the years my son was in high school he would enroll in one or more of this woman's classes, and it crossed my mind that someday he might ask her to write a letter of recommendation for his college applications. I knew all these things, and yet what I said to Dr. F was this:

"I need to take him to baseball practice. It's the first day and the coach will be mad if he's late."

There was a beat while this sharp, elegant person took my measure.

"This is an important test," she said, still with that faint, almost imperceptible accent. "He can play baseball any time."

No, he can't, I muttered to myself. As the words bumped against the censor in my head, I rued that I'd become the obnoxious helicopter parent I'd never thought I'd be.

In the third place, I learned that baseball is not the slow, boring game its critics complain about.

I was reading the autobiography of John Kruk, former MLB first baseman for the Padres, Phillies, and White Sox. In a book published in 1994, Kruk recounts an informal conversation with a fan: "I'm sitting in a restaurant . . . eating this big meal and maybe having a couple of beers and smoking a cigarette. A woman comes by the table. . . . She's getting all over me, saying that a professional athlete should take better care of himself. I lean back and I say to her, 'I ain't an athlete, lady. I'm a baseball player.'"

Stories of Kruk's gluttony are widespread — he was the only person on our team," said pitcher Curt Schilling, "who would wave down the hot dog vendor while sitting in the dugout between innings" — but in this case the mischievous Krukie was seriously underselling the game he played. Baseball has a reputation for being a lazy sport — the late sportswriter Pete Axthelm once called it "leisurely and pastoral" — but most events on a baseball field take place at the absolute limit of human physiological capabilities.

Take batting: once a fastball explodes out of the pitcher's hand, it crosses home plate in a little less than half a second, around 375-400 milliseconds. (An eyeblink, for comparison, lasts about the same time, 300 to 400 milliseconds.) Here's what goes on during that negligible scrap of time. The batter's first task, obviously, is to see the ball. This is a little more difficult than it might sound, because up until the moment he releases a baseball, a pitcher tries to shield it from the sight of the batter, whose eyes and brain must first, therefore, separate a small, white, speeding object from a cluttered visual background. Simply to "see" the ball, in other words, takes about 75 milliseconds, and during that time it has traveled about 10 feet closer.

What comes next is a miracle of adaptive physiology. Once eyes and brain, working together, say *ball!* the batter must immediately track its flight path and decide whether to swing. (Knowing when not to swing, say neuroscience researchers Jason Sherwin and Jordan Muraskin, is the hallmark of top hitters.) There's no time to spare. The brain needs around 200 milliseconds to choose between two simple options (such as when comparing pairs of single-digit numbers or different shades of colors), and by the time a batter commits (or not) to a swing, the ball is more than halfway home. Television cameras sometimes capture this miniscule, cognitive durée in the case of a brushback pitch. On screen, the batter appears strangely and alarmingly frozen until the ball is almost on top of him; he backs away — or drops to the ground — only at the last possible moment.

To the quarter of a second necessary for brain to say *ball!* and choose to swing (or not swing) at it, now add the time that the batter's motor cortex needs to initiate a muscular response to a stimulus (around 100 milliseconds), and then include the time necessary for his muscles to overcome the bat's inertia and swing it across the plate (another 100 milliseconds). It turns out that the performances of pitcher and hitter are surprisingly complementary: a fastball crosses home plate in about four-tenths of a second, while the batter needs a minimum of four-tenths of a second to hit it. Olympic runners are forever redefining the limits of legs and lungs, but as baseball nears its second centenary, batters aren't turning on fastballs any more quickly than their great-great-great grandfathers. They simply can't.

The athleticism displayed on the pitcher's mound is similarly astonishing. As a pitcher's arm starts forward, it accelerates to a speed of 1,200 rpm, about the same as the propeller of a Cessna taxiing for takeoff. No human motion is faster. As with batting, intrinsic to pitching is an extraordinary synchrony of brain, nerve, muscle, and bone. If you're performing simple actions with your hand such as turning on a light switch or opening a door, then getting the movements timed exactly right doesn't matter. But to throw a baseball as hard as you can and hit a dinner-plate-sized target almost 60 feet away, you must release the ball within a "launch window" of about two milliseconds. This is a sliver of time almost too small to be meaningful; even computers used in high-speed stock trading typically make their calculations more slowly. It hardly seems possible to act with such exquisite precision. Yet tens of thousands of baseball pitchers at all levels of the game perform this miracle more than 100 times a day, every day, from April through October. (To see what happens when a pitcher misses his launch window, watch Dr. Anthony Fauci throw out the first pitch at Nationals Park on opening day in 2020. The ball veers comically about 10 feet to the right of Sean Dolittle, ceremonial catcher for the occasion.)

How and why did humans ever learn to do this? An intriguing theory about the evolution of overhand throwing comes from the neurobiologist William Calvin. In a book called *The Throwing Madonna*, Calvin cites laboratory experiments that show overlapping neural pathways for two separate physical actions, speech and throwing. Such a coincidence, he says, is proof that these two different motor activities piggybacked, so to speak, on the same neurological network, perhaps even evolving together. Overhand throwing, says Calvin, "possibly promoted the first important lateralization of a function to the left brain, an ability to rapidly orchestrate muscles in novel sequences. And I'll bet that this muscle-sequencing lateralization, most noticeable these days as handedness, was what started up not only toolmaking but language."

Which brings me to my fourth and final point — baseball and poetry.

In the years my son pitched high school baseball, I was chair of the English Department at Emory University, and the first time I slipped out of the office early on game day I felt guilty. As I closed my door and walked past the administrative staff at their desks, I was seriously tempted to say I was headed to an afternoon meeting or to do research at the library. On a last-minute nudge from my better angel, however, I confessed that I was taking the afternoon off to watch my son's baseball game. I felt better for telling the truth, but I remember the occasion mainly for its ambient abrasiveness, an awkward friction such as occurs between social classes when someone who has control over his workplace hours makes use of that freedom in the face of people who lack similar options.

Breaches of fealty notwithstanding, that same scene played out twice a week for the ensuing five springs: February through May, Wednesdays and Fridays at 2 p.m., I ditched my job for the ballfield. I think now that if I had tried to balance work and play, literature and sport, more responsibly, I would have screwed up both. The road up and the road down, however, are sometimes the same, and, as if in accord with some benign karma, the more baseball I watched, the more I read up on it, and the more I read about the game and its players, the more I kept bumping into poetry and poets. The list of American writers who have played baseball or turned to it for subject matter reads like the members' directory in a literary Hall of Fame. I read Stephen Crane, Gregory Corso, Richard Eberhart, Robert Frost, Donald Hall, Ernest Hemingway, Richard Hugo, Marianne Moore, Robert Pinsky, Philip Roth, James Tate, Mark Twain, John Updike, Robert Penn Warren, Walt Whitman, Tom Wolfe, Paul Zimmer. Those readings turned into a new, undergraduate course called "Baseball and American Culture"; that course turned into a sequence of video lectures for the online education provider 2U, and, after that program ("Semester Online") was discontinued, the lectures turned into a nonfiction book, *Baseball in a Grain of Sand*. When the book was named a finalist for the Casey Award for the best baseball book of 2018, I felt like a character at the end of a comedy by Shakespeare, rewarded beyond measure for what looked all the while like folly.

The last four years my son played baseball, he pitched for a college located a thousand miles to the north; I saw only four or five games a year, almost always in March when the team made its annual, pre-conference southern swing, playing double headers in the Carolinas against Davidson, Wofford, Furman, or USC. The Atlanta Braves were a winning ball club in those days — 15 division championships from 1991 to 2010, including a crazy 14 titles in a row — but I rarely went downtown to see them play. Years of watching amateur baseball had made me impatient with the tawdry extravagances of MLB; it was insulting to have it assumed that I couldn't possibly be satisfied with the game unless every moment when the ball was not in play was stuffed with senseless intermezzi. I loved the amateur game with its bobbles and stumbles, its sparse crowds and raucous metal bleachers, its perfect imperfections. I can still see one of the Haney twins, both gifted athletes but inexplicably maladroit baseball players, executing a flawless pop-up slide a full body length short of third base, the faces of runner and fielder frozen in disbelief at having encountered each other too soon, and in the wrong place; I can see Doug Farrey's arrest-me red Corvette, an andropausal indulgence he parked during home games just behind the backscreen, where, season after season, foul balls rained down all around it, yet never once was it struck; or the scoreboard rising above the right field fence at Brook Run Park in the Atlanta suburb of Dunwoody, where the hopeless Clarkston "Angoras" were down 34-0, even as the home plate umpire, in a compassionate effort to stanch the torrent of runs, was bellowing *strike!* as soon as the ball left the Angoras' pitcher's hand; or klutzy Tyler Moore, gamely standing his ground in left field even as creeping drifts of evening fog smothered him from sight, scattered fans laughing as he vanished because everybody knew the poor kid couldn't catch a baseball even when he could see it, so it hardly mattered if he was lost inside a cloud bank; or Ben Smith, a gentle and warm-hearted man, warily peeking out from deep within the upper deck at Bush Field in New Haven, where, much too overwrought for society, he sat in shadowy solitude whenever his son Matt was on the mound; I can bring it all back and make it as vivid as it ever was, and as hallowed, before it all went away with the time, and I know now what A. Bartlett Giamatti, scholar of Renaissance literature and former president of Yale University, the National League, and Commissioner of Baseball, meant when, having reached the sobering, reflective age of 40, he wrote that the one thing he wished might last forever was a game, on a green field, in the sun.

Bill Gruber is emeritus professor of English at Emory University, author of multiple academic books and articles and two works of nonfiction, *On All Sides Nowhere* (Houghton Mifflin, 2002) and *Baseball in a Grain of Sand* (McFarland 2018). His essay, "Jocks, Herbs, the 1936 Yankees, Tea with Harold Bloom," appeared in *Sport Literate* in 2019.

Poetry

Obstructed View: Love and Baseball
Alinda Wasner

The day the elephants marched through Corktown and down Michigan Avenue, the crowds going wild inside Tiger Stadium with Gibby at bat and us in our obstructed view seats where we couldn't see diddly but what did that matter because we were crazy in love and had eyes only for each other even though our respective spouses and kids were there too, and God knows I've never been much for baseball — too much standing around — but that day I was giddy with the thought of extra innings and though you were initially a Padres fan, in the end, you were won over by the Champions and though we left before the crowds tore up half the turf for souvenirs, we followed the marching bands to the bar, pumping our fists when some rowdies turned over a cop car in the intersection, and later, much later, someone saw us kissing under a street lamp but what did that matter — at the time what mattered was the heat of the moment and though I've not seen you for years, and the stadium is gone, and no one who lives here can afford a ticket, every time I hear the roar of opening day, I fully expect to turn around and see you waiting to kiss my eyelids; and the hairs on the back of my neck stand up whenever I hear the crack of a bat on my grandson's team; so, I am reminded what a thrill it is to actually win from time to time and how love is in no way unlike a hot summer day at the circus, or the voice of Ernie Harwell, long dead now, over the radio and everyone cheering in the streets, revving their engines, windows down, bare feet on the dashboard as if we owned the world!

Alinda Dickinson Wasner's work has appeared in more than 40 small press print and online journals including *Ararat, Atlanta Review, Avatar, Comstock Review, Camroc Press Review, Crab Orchard, Evening Street,* and many others. She has won many literary prizes including several Tompkins Awards, Wittenberg University Writer's Award, Atlanta Review Prize, Mr. Cogito Press Award, Chicago Poetry Center juried prize, and a Prague Writer's fellowship, among others. In 2012 she received second place in Ireland's International Poetry Prize out of 2000 entrants. She has published a collection of poetry, *Still Burning* (Ex Libris), and two chapbooks. Another collection is forthcoming from Mayapple Press in 2023. She lives and writes in metro Detroit.

Poetry

An Appearance of Brightness
Matthew Sisson

The Egyptians had Ra.
The Greeks, Apollo.
They knew where their
bread was buttered.
Cole Porter worshipped
the sun too. He wrote
Night and Day. I love
Ella Fitzgerald's
version. Sinatra's too.

Now we know light is
electromagnetic radiation.
Behaves like particles
and waves bouncing around
Colorado's furs and aspens.
Wilting my brother-in-law's
tomato plants in Indianapolis.

She left —
Think of it this way:
It was like being hit by
a Roger Clemens fastball
under the bright lights of
a night game at Fenway.

Matthew Sisson's poetry has appeared in journals ranging from the *Harvard Review Online*, to *JAMA The Journal of the American Medical Association*. He has been nominated for a Pushcart Prize, and read his work on NPR's "On Point." His first book, *Please, Call Me Moby*, was published by the Pecan Grove Press.

Poetry

Autumn Field in a Pascagoula Sundown
Jeffrey Alfier

The boy who knows he's late to supper
    is over at the off-season ballpark,

coastal autumn still holding the tepid air
    that ended the final inning.

Like someone musing a trespass, his fingers
    thread the chain-link by the home team dugout.

His eyes drift to a hawk chasing a minion —
    some smaller set of wings that seek a corner

to assemble a nest, perhaps under the overhang
    that shades the vacant stands,

before those wings are astonished by lithe talons,
    the boy's eyes adjusting to the dark.

Jeffrey Alfier's most recent book, *The Shadow Field*, was published by Louisiana Literature Journal & Press (2020). Journal credits include *Carolina Quarterly*, *Copper Nickel*, *Faultline*, *Hotel Amerika*, *New York Quarterly*, *Penn Review*, *Southern Poetry Review*, and *Vassar Review*.

SPORT Literate

BACK IN THE FALL

SPORT LITERATE HOPES TO BE BACK IN MAILBOXES THIS FALL (MAYBE EARLY NEXT YEAR). WE NEED READERS AND WRITERS.

DISCOVER OPPORTUNITIES FOR BOTH ONLINE...

WWW.SPORTLITERATE.ORG

What's Your Story?

We can handle your truth

Who's on First
This first-person essay begins each issue. Mark Wukas led off "Spring Eats 1997" with "Running With Ghosts," an essay subsequently recognized in the *Best American Sports Writing* (*BASW*) anthology. Michael McColly's "Christmas City, U.S.A." won a creative nonfiction award from the Illinois Arts Council back in the day. Frank Soos was recognized in *BASW* in 2013 for his lead-off essay, "Another Kind of Loneliness." *BASW 2017* gave a nod to Laura Legge's essay, "The Responsible Player." And Virginia Ottley Craighill's essay, "The Lost Cause," was anthologized in *BASW 2019* and earned a "notable" nod in *Best American Essays (BAE) 2019*. Most recently, Anthony D'Aries earned a *BAE* nod in 2021 for "No Man's Land."

SL Travel
As that stranger in a strange land, what did you learn on the road? What's the leisurely life like over there? Robert Parker's travel piece, "The Running of the Bull," was recognized in *Best American Essays (BAE) 2006*.

Personal Essay

We're hip to all the nonfiction forms — nature writing, immersion journalism — whatever floats your prose. More than 30 *Sport Literate* writers have been cited in the annual *BAE* and the *BASW* collections. Mark Pearson's essay, "The Short History of an Ear," was our first to make the latter anthology's pages. Cinthia Ritchie's "Running" appeared there in 2013. We've got enough "Best Americans" over 26 years to fill out a football squad. Check them out on page 13. Six of our writers earned six more in 2020.

Poetry

Frank Van Zant handles the poetry. You might peruse the verse here and take in a back issue or two. Send up to three poems at a time our way, and we'll get it to Frank.

Interviews

We hope these are just good conversations with smart people. In past issues, we've featured Chicago footballers (Bear, Chris Zorich, and Cardinal, Marshall Goldberg), sportswriters (Bill Gleason, Robert Lipsyte, and Dave Zirin), and a poet (Jack Ridl). Query with suggestions.

SL Shorts

In our "20th Anniversary Issue," we offered 11 quick hits of flash nonfiction. In a contest judged by Dinty W. Moore, Robert Wallace took home the $500 prize for his short, "Rush Lake." We reprised that contest in 2020, with Jay Lesandrini selecting Hal Ackerman's short, "Concrete Charlie and the Golden Boy," for the $1,000 prize. Send us your clean shorts (meaning crisp and properly proofed) of 1,000 words or less.

All submissions come online now through the
Submittable link on our website.

www.sportliterate.org

Sport Literate

PUSHING PROGRESS

In April 1947, Jackie Robinson broke the color barrier in Major League Baseball when he was "called up" from Canada to the Brooklyn Dodgers. MLB, rightfully, celebrated the 75th anniversary of that occasion near the start of this year's season. But as the summer of 2022 heated up, the U.S. Supreme Court rolled back Constitutional rights for women and appear poised for a 1950s nostalgia that would threaten voting rights, marriage equality, and other civil liberties. Baseball fans opposed to a United States of Apartheid should take note. And push back.